THE RED BOOK

PIANO/VOCAL/CHORDS

TEN YEARS OF POP MUSIC HISTORY

1990-2000

REMEMBERING THE '90s

Project Manager: Carol Cuellar
Art Design: Jorge Paredes
Text By: Fucini Productions, Inc.

CONTENTS

CONTENTS

CELINE DION

Music runs in Celine Dion's family. The internationally acclaimed recording artist grew up in the little town of Charlemagne in Quebec, Canada. Celine was the youngest of 14 children, all of them talented in music. Her parents, both musicians themselves, owned a club in town. On weekends, the entire Dion clan would entertain local residents at the club.

Celine's soaring natural musical genius set her apart even in her talented family. At the age of 12 she recorded a demo tape of a French song she composed with her mother and one of her brothers. Her family took the tape to Rene Angelil, a music promoter. He was so taken with Celine's honeyed voice that he mortgaged his house to finance the recording of her first album.

History would prove Mr. Angelil to be a sharp judge of talent. After establishing herself as a star in French-speaking Quebec, Celine released her first English-language album, *Unison,* in April 1990. Her big break came when she recorded the soundtrack for the animated film *Beauty and the Beast* in 1992, a recording that won both an Academy Award and a Grammy Award.

Respected as one of the world's hardest-working artists, Celine released three albums between 1992 and 1994. Her career reached another outstanding milestone in 1996 with the release of *Falling Into You,* which became the best-selling album of the year, topped the charts in 11 countries, and then won a Grammy for good measure.

Just when it seemed Celine's incredible career could soar no higher, she recorded "My Heart Will Go On," the theme song from the blockbuster film *Titanic.* The eloquently haunting sound of Celine's vocals, as deep and mysterious as the sea itself, provided an unforgettable musical backdrop to this tale of star-crossed lovers on an ill-fated ship. Released in November 1997, the *Titanic* soundtrack sold more than 27 million copies. Celine's album, *Let's Talk About Love,* which also featured the Academy Award-winning film theme song, went on to match the incredible sales figure of the *Titanic* soundtrack.

As 1999 drew to a close, the Canadian Recording Industry Association named Celine the country's best-selling recording artist of the twentieth century. The girl from little Charlemagne had indeed come a very long way.

*NSYNC

Mother knows best—at least when it comes to naming a superstar pop group. When Justin Timberlake and his four buddies were wondering what to name their new band in the mid-'90s, his mom suggested *NSYNC. The guys liked the name instantly because it expressed the great harmony between their singing and dancing. Only later did they learn that Justin's mother had created the catchy moniker by taking the last letter from each boy's first name: JustiN, ChriS (Kirkpatrick), JoeY (Fatone, Jr.), LansteN (Bass), and J.C. (Chasez).

By 1998, music fans all over the world would know and love the name *NSYNC thanks to the group's smooth songs and awesome live performances. True to their name, *NSYNC serves up a great blend of music and choreography. This fabulous five-some does more than go through the motions when they dance. Like five bundles of energy, they fill a stage with dazzling motion as they work their way through routines with passion and precision.

*NSYNC's debut single, the pop-soul tune "I Want You Back," stormed into the Top 10 of the Hot 100 chart in 1998. The group showed its musical versatility by following this song with the pulsating dance-floor hit "Tearin' Up My Heart." Returning home to the States in the spring of 1998 after a successful European tour, *NSYNC released its self-titled album, which has gone multi-platinum. In 1999, the *NSYNC express continued to roll with hits like "For the Girl Who Has Everything."

Despite their young ages—Justin was only 14 when the group started—*NSYNC has taken their quick rise to the top of the music world in stride. Maybe that's because the boys were already seasoned pros when the group was formed. Justin and J.C. had been regulars on the "The Mickey Mouse Club," Chris had worked for Universal Studios, and Joey had appeared in movies like *Matinee* and *Once Upon a Time in America.*

*NSYNC got its start when Justin and J.C. shared their dreams of starting a music group. They soon brought the other three members into their plan. Right from the start, the five-some felt they had the right chemistry to make it. After all, they were totally *NSYNC!

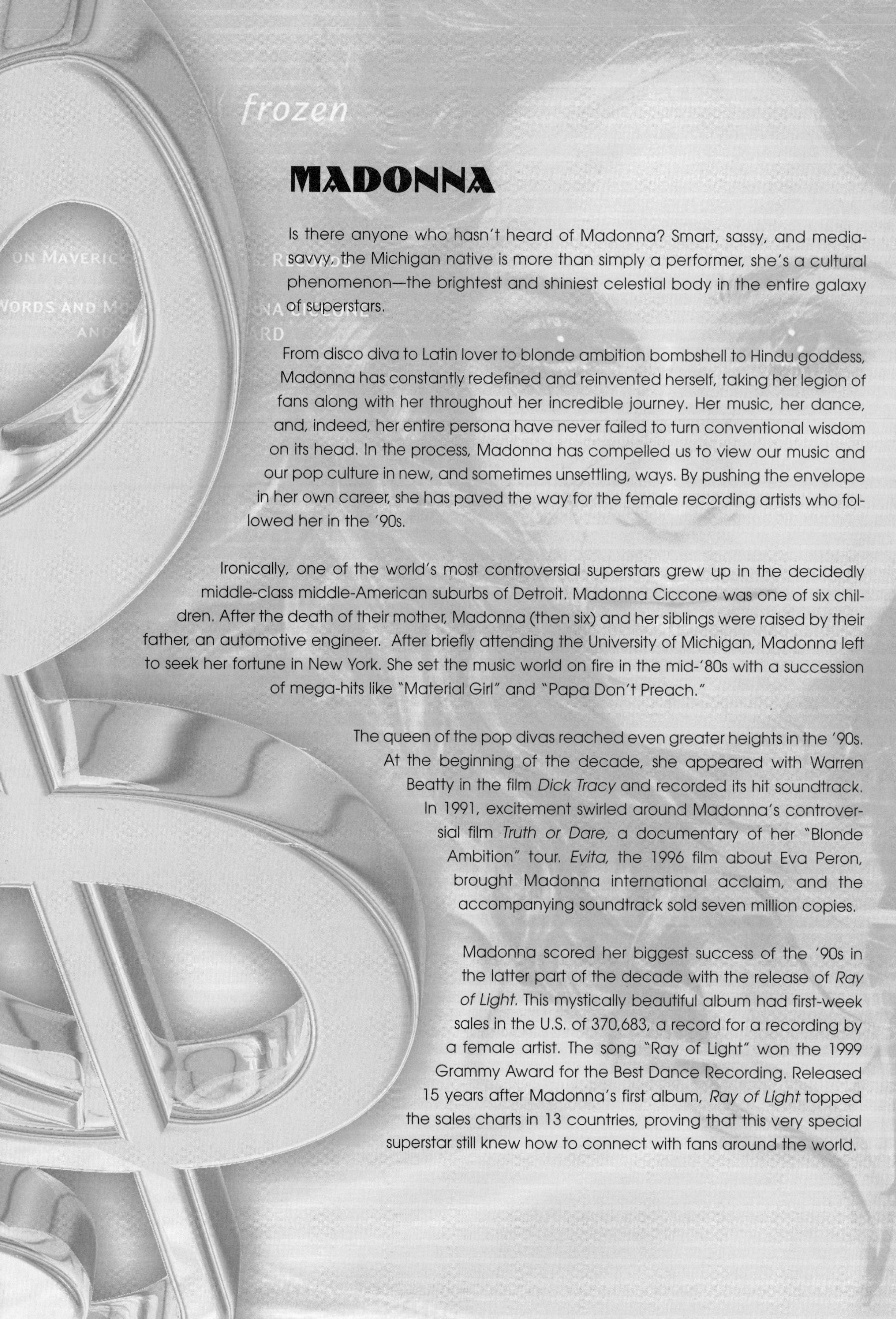

frozen

MADONNA

Is there anyone who hasn't heard of Madonna? Smart, sassy, and media-savvy, the Michigan native is more than simply a performer, she's a cultural phenomenon—the brightest and shiniest celestial body in the entire galaxy of superstars.

From disco diva to Latin lover to blonde ambition bombshell to Hindu goddess, Madonna has constantly redefined and reinvented herself, taking her legion of fans along with her throughout her incredible journey. Her music, her dance, and, indeed, her entire persona have never failed to turn conventional wisdom on its head. In the process, Madonna has compelled us to view our music and our pop culture in new, and sometimes unsettling, ways. By pushing the envelope in her own career, she has paved the way for the female recording artists who followed her in the '90s.

Ironically, one of the world's most controversial superstars grew up in the decidedly middle-class middle-American suburbs of Detroit. Madonna Ciccone was one of six children. After the death of their mother, Madonna (then six) and her siblings were raised by their father, an automotive engineer. After briefly attending the University of Michigan, Madonna left to seek her fortune in New York. She set the music world on fire in the mid-'80s with a succession of mega-hits like "Material Girl" and "Papa Don't Preach."

The queen of the pop divas reached even greater heights in the '90s. At the beginning of the decade, she appeared with Warren Beatty in the film *Dick Tracy* and recorded its hit soundtrack. In 1991, excitement swirled around Madonna's controversial film *Truth or Dare,* a documentary of her "Blonde Ambition" tour. *Evita,* the 1996 film about Eva Peron, brought Madonna international acclaim, and the accompanying soundtrack sold seven million copies.

Madonna scored her biggest success of the '90s in the latter part of the decade with the release of *Ray of Light.* This mystically beautiful album had first-week sales in the U.S. of 370,683, a record for a recording by a female artist. The song "Ray of Light" won the 1999 Grammy Award for the Best Dance Recording. Released 15 years after Madonna's first album, *Ray of Light* topped the sales charts in 13 countries, proving that this very special superstar still knew how to connect with fans around the world.

MARIAH CAREY

The only recording artist in history whose first five singles reached No.1 on the Hot 100 Singles chart . . . The biggest first-week sales ever for a single (271,000 copies of "Heartbreaker" in 1999) . . . More No.1 hits than any other female recording artist (14) . . . If there's a benchmark for success in music, it's safe to assume that Mariah Carey has established it.

Mariah's magic has bedazzled fans in every corner of the world. The beautiful songstress from Long Island has sold more than 120 million albums and singles worldwide in the '90s, earning an astonishing 84 gold, platinum, and multi-platinum certifications. It's no wonder Mariah is regarded as the female recording artist of the '90s by many critics.

In many respects, Mariah has provided us with a soundtrack to the '90s. She came out with her debut album, *Mariah*, in the decade's first year, winning two Grammy Awards. Her final album of the decade, *Rainbow*, was released in 1999. In between came works like *Emotions*, *Music Box*, *Daydream*, and *Butterfly* that reflected the pulse of the decade that ushered in the Information Age.

Like the '90s, Mariah and her music have celebrated diversity. Her work embraces a tapestry of musical fabrics, including pop, soul, gospel, R&B, hip-hop, and even traditional Christmas carols like "Silent Night." Mariah's stunning seven-octave voice has allowed her to go where singers of lesser abilities would fear to tread. Only a singer of Mariah's range and versatility could record No. 1 hits with artists as diverse as Whitney Houston, Jermaine Dupri, and Boyz II Men. Mariah's vocal prowess can thrill us with its swoops and seductive rhythms in songs like "Fantasy" and then melt our hearts the next moment with the delicate vulnerability it conveys in her unplugged version of the Jackson Five's "I'll Be There."

Born in 1970, Mariah was raised by her mother, a former singer with the New York City Opera. Mariah began practicing opera songs with her mother when she was only three. As a child, she knew that one day she would be a star—but even the confident and talented little girl from Long Island could not have known how brightly her fame would shine over the decade of the '90s.

JIM BRICKMAN

From 32-year-old businessman to new-age recording star, that describes the incredible career path of Jim Brickman. The Cleveland, Ohio native was making his living composing themes and jingles for corporate clients in the early '90s when he decided to try something new. Renting time at a local studio, he sat at a piano and recorded some original compositions. Jim sent his demo tapes to program directors and other executives at easy-listening radio stations. Impressed with his warm melodies and sublime styling, the radio people wrote back saying that they would love to play his music. Being an astute businessman, Jim then forwarded these letters along with demo tapes to recording companies. This led to a record contract, and in 1994 he released his debut album, *No Words.*

Despite the early encouragement from radio execs, getting airplay for an instrumental album by an unknown artist wasn't easy, but Jim worked hard to market his new recording. He visited radio stations in person, giving free in-studio concerts and listener-appreciation shows. Soon the soothing strains of his piano were being heard on radios across the U.S. With the airplay came fans. In 1995, the title song from Jim's second album, *By Heart,* became his first Top 20 hit. The album itself was later certified gold, as were Jim's next two albums, *Picture This* and *The Gift.*

In 1997, Jim worked with country star Martina McBride to record "Valentine," a song that climbed up the country and adult contemporary charts and went on to become a standard request on Cupid's favorite holiday. Later, Jim gave a musical tradition to another holiday when the title song from his Christmas album, *The Gift,* became a Yuletide favorite.

Although he got started "late" as a performer, Jim has emerged as the kind of artist who wins enormous respect and affection from his peers. Maybe that's why so many of the music world's leading lights seem to enjoy performing with him. This was very evident in Jim's fifth album, *Destiny,* which included collaborations with guests Carly Simon, Michael W. Smith, Pam Tillis, Herb Alpert, and others. Like fans everywhere, these artists have fallen in love with Jim's gentle piano style. The business world's loss has been the music lover's gain.

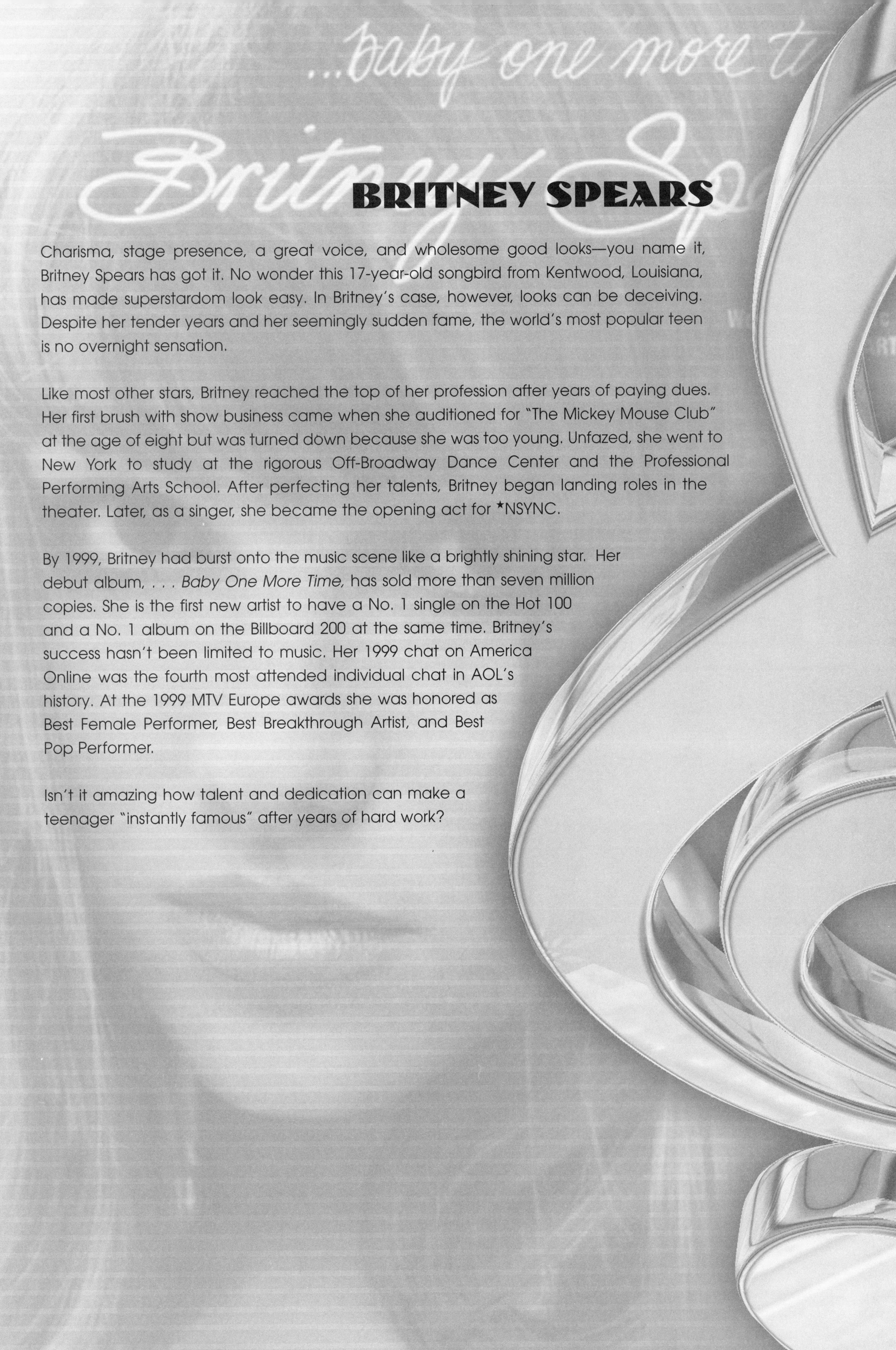

BRITNEY SPEARS

Charisma, stage presence, a great voice, and wholesome good looks—you name it, Britney Spears has got it. No wonder this 17-year-old songbird from Kentwood, Louisiana, has made superstardom look easy. In Britney's case, however, looks can be deceiving. Despite her tender years and her seemingly sudden fame, the world's most popular teen is no overnight sensation.

Like most other stars, Britney reached the top of her profession after years of paying dues. Her first brush with show business came when she auditioned for "The Mickey Mouse Club" at the age of eight but was turned down because she was too young. Unfazed, she went to New York to study at the rigorous Off-Broadway Dance Center and the Professional Performing Arts School. After perfecting her talents, Britney began landing roles in the theater. Later, as a singer, she became the opening act for *NSYNC.

By 1999, Britney had burst onto the music scene like a brightly shining star. Her debut album, *. . . Baby One More Time,* has sold more than seven million copies. She is the first new artist to have a No. 1 single on the Hot 100 and a No. 1 album on the Billboard 200 at the same time. Britney's success hasn't been limited to music. Her 1999 chat on America Online was the fourth most attended individual chat in AOL's history. At the 1999 MTV Europe awards she was honored as Best Female Performer, Best Breakthrough Artist, and Best Pop Performer.

Isn't it amazing how talent and dedication can make a teenager "instantly famous" after years of hard work?

GLORIA ESTEFAN

Recorded by GLORIA ESTEFAN on Epic Records

Words and Music by GLORIA ESTEFAN and DIANE WARREN

The Latin explosion that reshaped popular music in the U.S. in the late '90s actually got started more than a decade earlier. Long before Ricky Martin came along, Gloria Estefan and the Miami Sound Machine were giving North Americans their first taste of the modern Latin music with hits like "Conga."

There couldn't have been a better ambassador for the Latin sound than Gloria. Attractive and talented, she has the kind of natural charisma that automatically captivates people. She also has a heart that's as big and warm as her music. Her Gloria Estefan Charities has been widely recognized for its work helping children and the underprivileged.

Emilio Estefan undoubtedly appreciated these qualities when he met Gloria at a wedding in 1975. Performing at the reception, Emilio coaxed his future wife on stage to sing two songs and later offered her a job with his band. By the '80s, the couple's Miami Sound Machine was energizing North American music with a new Latin beat.

In 1990 Gloria's career was nearly derailed after her group's bus was involved in an accident that left her with a broken vertebra. Gloria came back one year later better than ever. Her 1991 solo album, *Into the Light,* showed a more developed pop style than her earlier works. This was followed by *Mi Tierra* in 1993, a collection of Spanish songs that went platinum in the U.S. and became the best-selling album ever in Spain.

With the 1996 release of her *Destiny* album, Gloria fused Latin influences with adult contemporary sounds. The result was a lively collection of songs, including "Reach," the 1996 Summer Olympic Games anthem. Gloria performed the song at the games' closing ceremonies. Her 1998 album, *Gloria,* was another successful blend of different musical influences—in this case, dance with strong Latin rhythms.

On January 31, 1999, Gloria performed during the half-time show at the Super Bowl, which was held in her hometown of Miami. This made Gloria the first recording artist to appear at two Super Bowls. (She performed at the 1992 game.) It's fitting that Gloria holds a "Super Bowl record." She has been a real winner on and off the stage for two decades.

GLORIA

estefan

ENRIQUE IGLESIAS

Born in Spain and raised in Miami, Enrique Iglesias was nurtured by the rich musical traditions of three cultures: Hispanic, European, and American. This diversity, along with Enrique's phenomenal natural talent, is evident in his recordings and concerts, which have made him an international superstar.

The son of the beloved singer Julio Iglesias, Enrique released his first album, *Enrique Iglesias,* in 1995. He followed it two years later with his second album, *Vivir.* Together, the two Spanish-language albums sold more than 10.5 million copies. Singles from Enrique's albums have been No. 1 on the Billboard charts in the U.S. and 18 other countries. By the end of the '90s, Enrique's gentle yet passionate vocal style had earned him an amazing 116 platinum records, 227 gold records, and 26 international awards, including a 1996 Grammy for Best Latin Performer.

Enrique's magic isn't limited to the recording studio. His concerts are celebrations of life, love, and music. The charismatic and enchanting singer is rarely confined by the physical boundaries of the stage. He reaches out to his audience literally and physically, inviting them to share the emotions of his deeply personal performance. Fans throughout the world have responded to Enrique's beckoning. In 1997, his *Vivir* tour of 78 concerts in 13 countries won rave reviews and was attended by 720,000 people.

Being dashingly handsome hasn't hurt Enrique's popularity either. With his bedroom eyes and classic features, his face has graced the covers of more than 250 magazines. Enrique also appeared on almost 200 television programs in 23 countries during the '90s. In 1999, he received even wider exposure when his hit song "Bailamos" was featured in the film *Wild Wild West.*

Given his immense popularity and famous father, it surprised many people to learn that Enrique was rejected by several major record labels when he began his career at the age of 16 (in 1991) without the knowledge of his family. Despite the initial setbacks, Enrique persisted until his unique blend of music earned him a place among the superstars of the recording world. Good things do indeed happen to those who wait—and continue to apply their natural talent.

From the Original Motion Picture Soundtrack "THE THREE MUSKETEERS"

ALL FOR LOVE

Written by
BRYAN ADAMS, ROBERT JOHN "MUTT" LANGE
and MICHAEL KAMEN

Verse:
A
D
Dsus
Rod:
hold. 2. When there's love in - side,
then there's a rea - son why.
Bryan: I swear I'll al - ways be strong.
Rod: then it's love you take.
(3.) Sting: I'll be the fire in your night.
D
D/F♯
G
Both: I'll be the world that pro - tects you
I'll prove to you we be - long.
All: I'll be there when you need me
I will de - fend I will fight.
D/A
A
Asus
A
from the wind and the rain, from the hurt and the pain.
when hon - or's at stake, this vow I will make:
cresc.

Chorus:
D Em7 D/F♯ N.C. D/F♯ G
All: Let's make it
that it's
all for one, all for love.
mf
Em7 D/A
Let the one you hold be the one you want, the one you
A D/F♯ G Bm A D/F♯ G
need. 'Cause when it's all for one, it's one for all. When there's
Em7 D/F♯ G D/A
some - one that you know, then just let your feel - ings show and make it

1.
D.S. 𝄋
2.
G D/F♯ Em7 A
D
Dsus
D
all for one, all for love.
all,
Bryan: 3. When it's love you make,
dim.
mp
Bridge:
Bm
G
Em7 D/F♯ G A
Don't lay our love to rest, 'cause we could stand up to the test. We've got
Bm
D/F♯
G Asus A
ev - 'ry - thing and more than we had planned, more than the riv -
Bm
D/F♯
G
A
- ers that run the land, we've got it all in our hands.

1.
G
Em7
Dsus
D
(Instrumental solo . . .
Dsus
D
2.
Asus
A
N.C.
. . . end solo)
Now, it's
Chorus:
G
Em7
all for___ one, all for love.___
Let the one you hold be the one you___
D/A
A
D/F♯
G
Bm
A
D/F♯
want, the one you___ need. 'Cause when it's all for___ one, it's one for all.___

G
Em7
D/F♯
When there's some - one that you know, then just
G
D/A
G/B
D/F♯
let your feel - ings show. When there's some - one that you want, when there's
G
D/A
Em
N.C.
some - one that you need, let's make it all, all for one,
slower
a tempo
Gm7
Gm(maj7)
Gm/A
D
D(2)
and all for love.
mp slower
a tempo
rit. e dim.
p

ALL I WANNA DO

Words and Music by SHERYL CROW, WYN COOPER,
BILL BOTTRELL, DAVID BAERWALD and KEVIN GILBERT

E7
a - pro - pos of noth - ing. He says his name is Wil - liam, but I'm
C7
D9
sure he's Bill or Bil - ly or Mac or Bud - dy. 2. But he's
Verses 2 & 3:
E7
plain ug - ly to me and I won - der if he's ev - er had
3. See additional lyrics.
C7
D9
E7
a day of fun in his whole life. We are drink - ing beer at

C7
D9
noon on Tues-day in a bar that fac - es a gi - ant car wash. And the
E7
good peo - ple of the world are wash - ing their cars on their lunch break,
C7
D9
hos - ing and scrub-bing as best they can in skirts and suits.
Bridge:
A13
B♭13
They drive their shin - y Dat - suns and Bu - icks

A13
B♭13
A13
back to the phone
com-pan-y, the re-cord store too._
Well, they're_ noth-ing like
Chorus:
E7
Bil-ly and me._ 'Cause all I wan-na do is have some fun,___ I got a feel-
C7
D9
E7
- ing I'm not the on - ly one. All I wan-na do is have some fun,_
C7
D9
___ I got a feel - ing I'm not the on - ly one. All I wan-na

E7
To Coda
C7
do is have some fun,
un - til the sun comes up o - ver
1. B7
E7
San - ta Mon - i - ca Boul - e - vard.
C7
D9
2. B7
San - ta Mon - i - ca Boul - e - vard.
E7
C7
D9
3

E7 C7 D9

Bridge:

A13 B♭13 A13

Oth-er-wise_ the bar___ is ours, and the day and the night and the

B♭13 A13

car wash too.___ The match-es and the Buds and the

B♭13 A13 *D.S.* 𝄋 *al Coda*

clean___ and dir-ty cars, the sun and the moon. But all I wan-na

Coda
C7
D9
E7
I've got a feel - ing the par - ty has just be - gun. All I wan - na
do is have some fun, I won't tell you that you're the on -
- ly one. All I wan - na do is have some fun, un - til the
sun comes up o - ver San - ta Mon - i - ca Boul - e - vard,

Verse 3:
I like a good beer buzz early in the morning,
And Billy likes to peel the labels from his bottles of Bud
And shred them on the bar.
Then he lights every match in an oversized pack,
Letting each one burn down to his thick fingers
Before blowing and cursing them out.
And he's watching the Buds as they spin on the floor.
A happy couple enters the bar dancing dangerously close to one another.
The bartender looks up from his want ads.
(To Chorus:)

ALL MY LIFE

Words and Music by
RORY BENNETT and
JO JO HAILEY

Verse:
Db
Ab/C
Bbm7
Gb
Ab
1. I will nev-er find an-oth-er lov-er sweet-er than you, sweet-er than you. And
I will nev-er find an-oth-er lov-er more pre-cious than you, more pre-cious than you. Girl, you are
Ebm7
close to me, you're like my moth-er; close to me, you're like my fa-ther; close to me, you're like my sis-ter; close to me, you're like my broth-er.
2. See additional lyrics
You are the on - ly one, you're my ev-'ry-thin', and for you this song I sing. In

Chorus:
E♭m
D♭
A♭/C
D♭
A♭/C
B♭m7
all my life, I pray for some-one like you. And
E♭m
D♭
A♭/C
D♭
Fm
B♭m7
I thank God that I fi-nal-ly found you.
E♭m
D♭
A♭/C
F/A
F/C
B♭m
A♭
All my life, I pray for some-one like you, and I
G♭
A♭
B♭m
A♭
B♭m
A♭/C
D♭
A♭/C
B♭m
A♭
hope that you feel the same way too. Yes, I

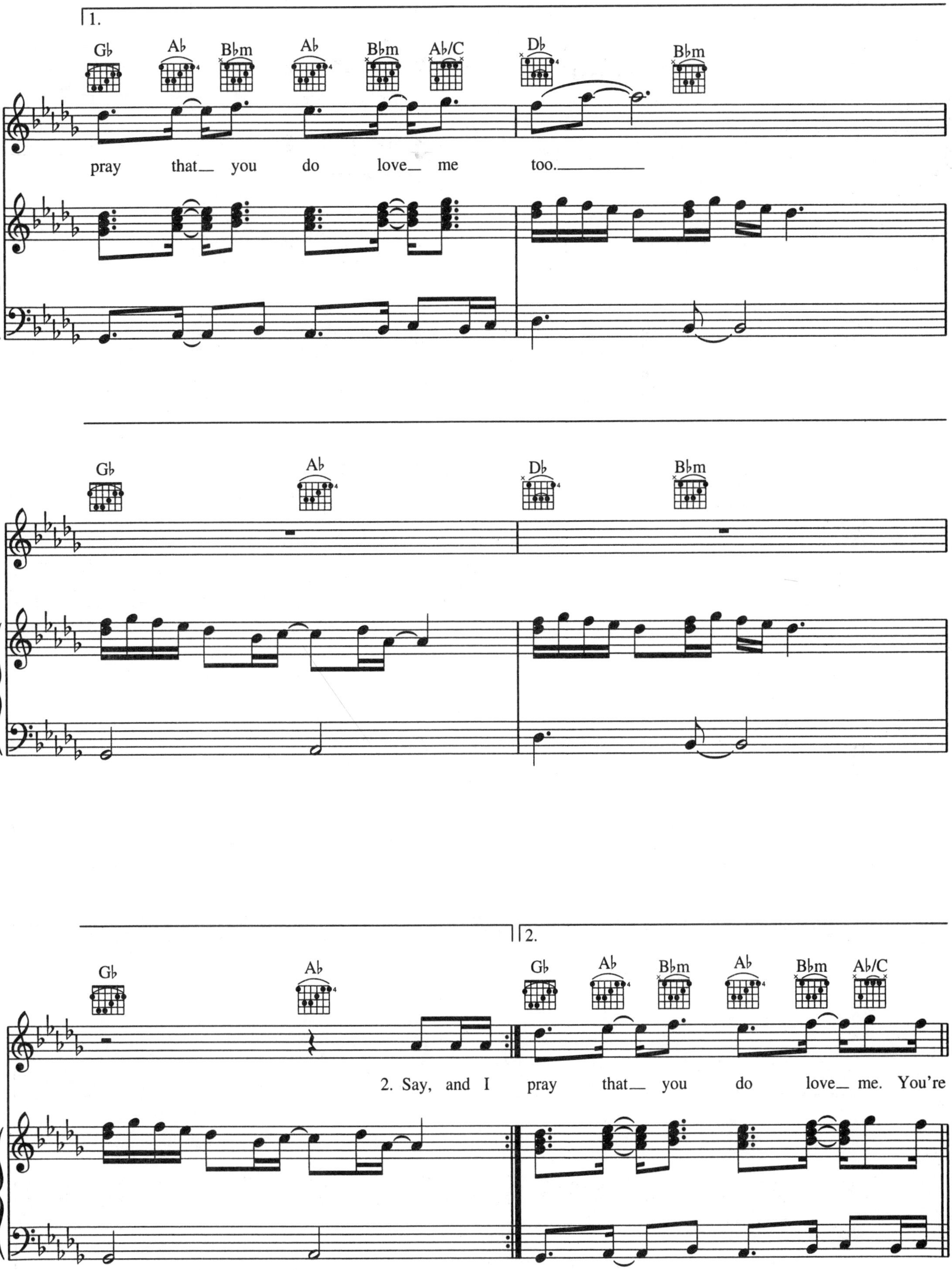
1.
G♭ A♭ B♭m A♭ B♭m A♭/C D♭ B♭m
pray that_ you do love_ me too.
G♭ A♭ D♭ B♭m
G♭ A♭
2.
G♭ A♭ B♭m A♭ B♭m A♭/C
2. Say, and I pray that_ you do love_ me. You're

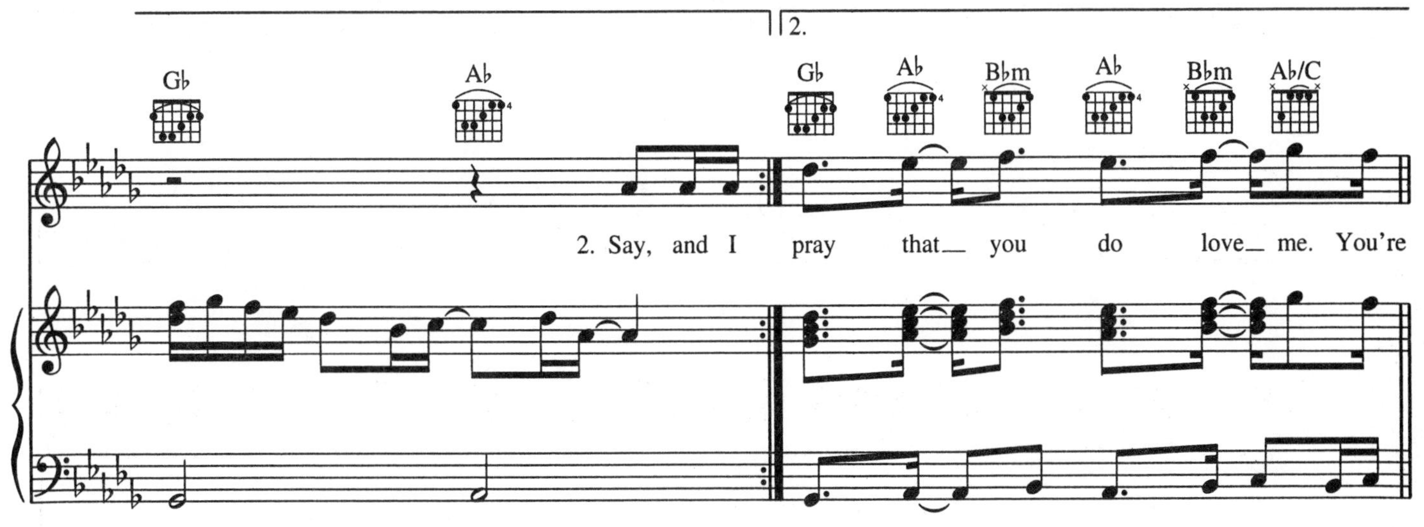

Bridge:
Ebm Ab/C F F/A Bbm Bb/D
all that_ I ev - er know;_ when you smile_ on my face,_ all I see_ is a glow._ You turn_
Ebm Ab/C F F/A Bbm Bb/D
___ my life_ a - round,_ you pick_ me up___ when I___ was down._ You're
Ebm Ab/C F F/A Bbm Bb/D
all that I ev - er know; when you smile, my face glow. You pick me up when I was down. Say, you
Ebm Ab/C F F/A Bbm Ab
all that I ev - er know; when you smile, my face glow. You pick me up when I was down. And I

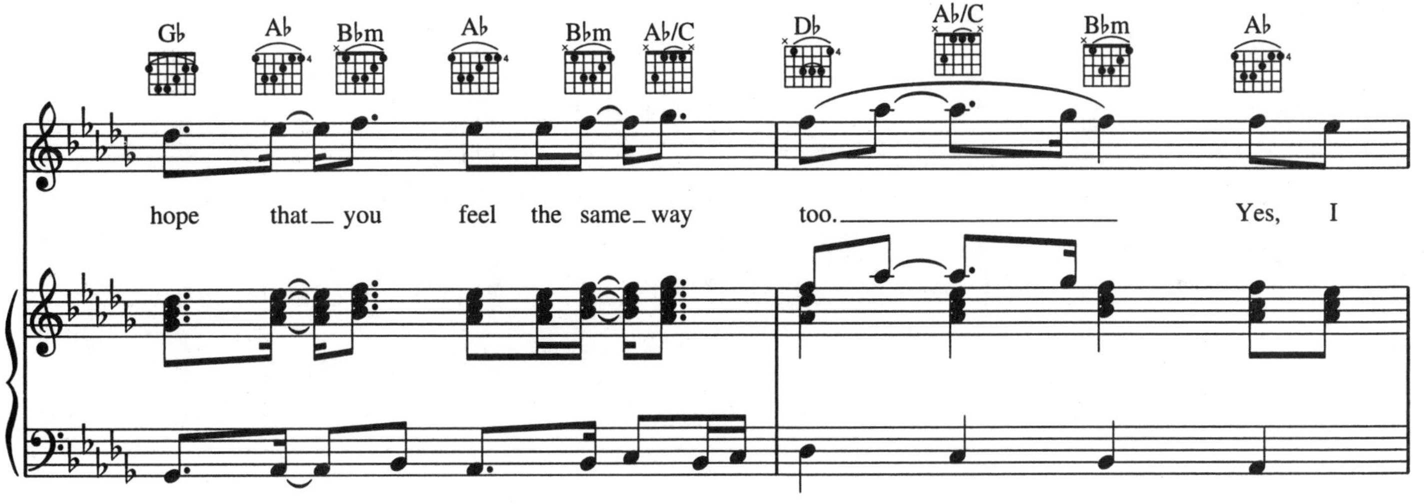
Gb Ab Bbm Ab Bbm Ab/C Db Ab/C Bbm Ab
hope that you feel the same way too. Yes, I

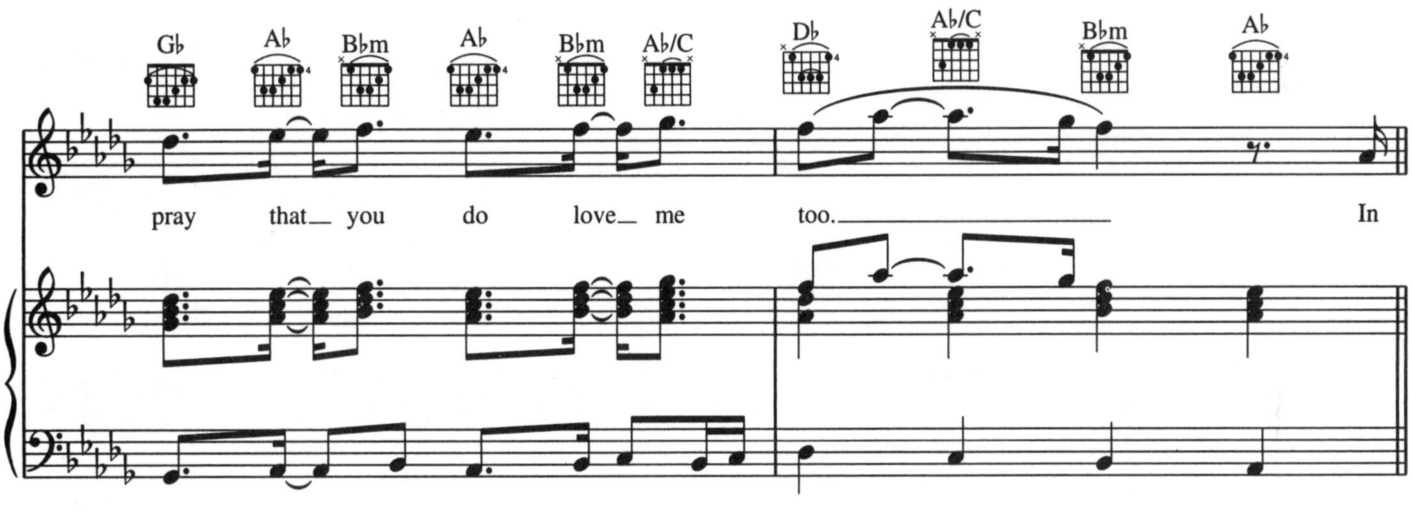
Gb Ab Bbm Ab Bbm Ab/C Db Ab/C Bbm Ab
pray that you do love me too. In

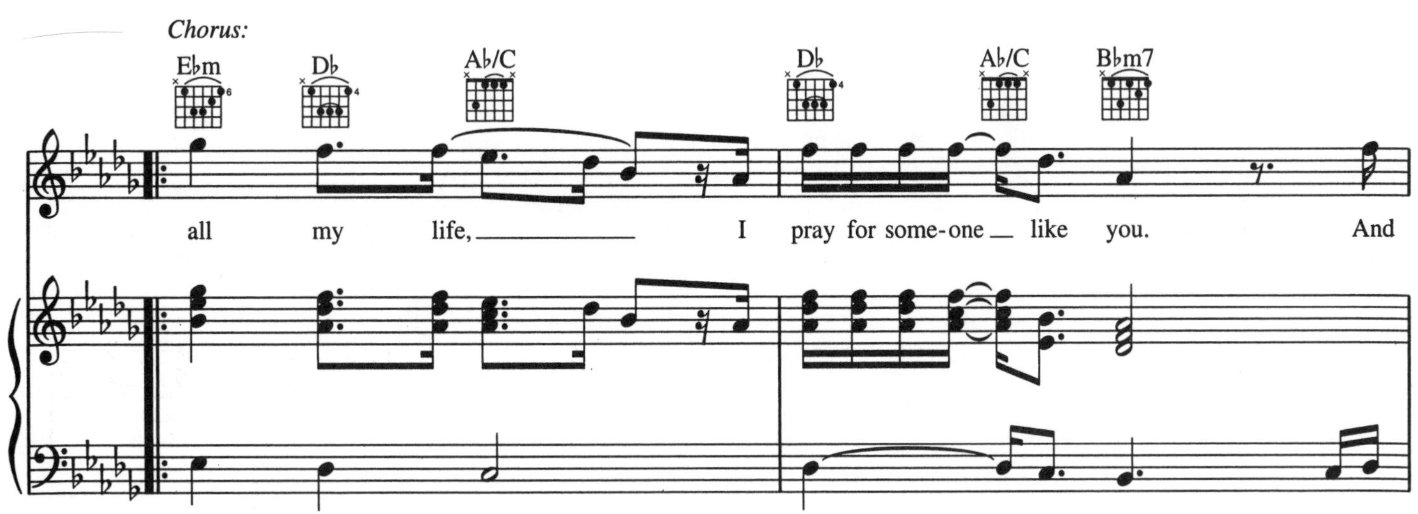
Chorus:
Ebm Db Ab/C Db Ab/C Bbm7
all my life, I pray for some-one like you. And

Verse 2:
Say, and I promise to never fall in love with a stranger.
You're all I'm thinkin', love, I praise the Lord above
For sendin' me your love, I cherish every hug.
I really love you so much.
(To Chorus:)

AS LONG AS YOU LOVE ME

By
MAX MARTIN

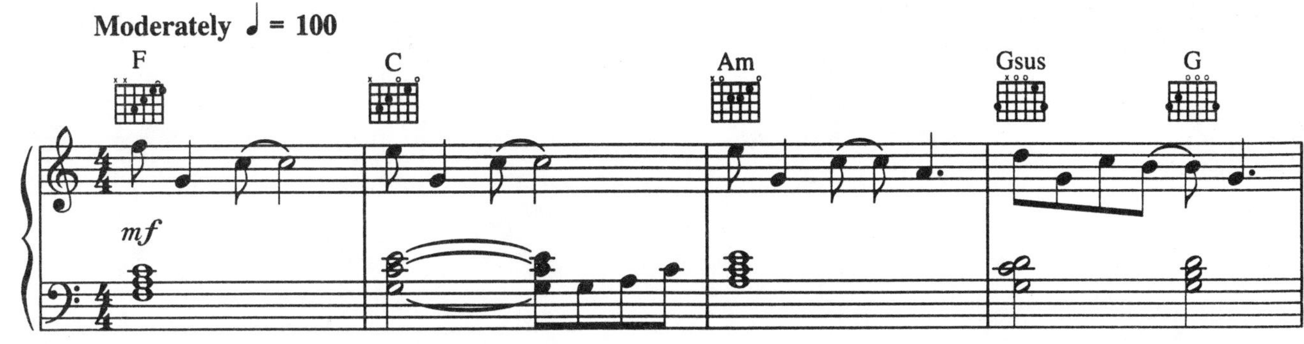

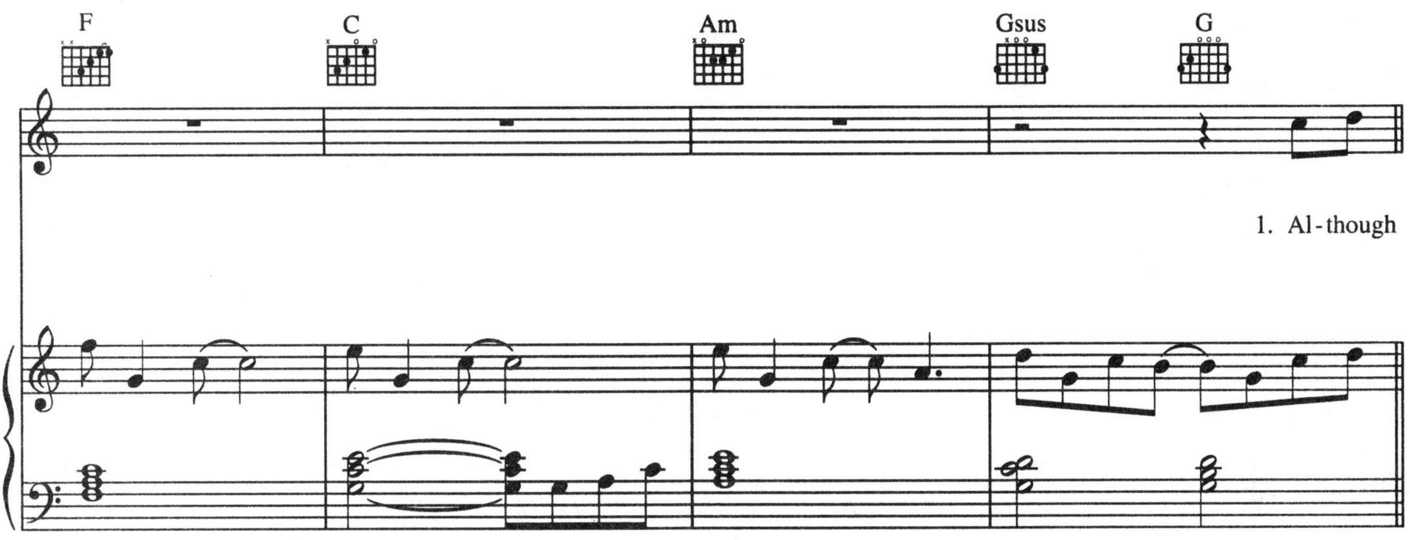

G
C
G/B
Am
leav - ing my life in your hands.
Peo - ple say I'm cra - zy and that
F
G
C
I am blind
risk - ing it all in a glance.
Verses 2 & 3:
Am
F
2. How you got me blind is still a mys - ter - y,
I
3. Ev - 'ry lit - tle thing that you have said and done
G
C
G/B
Am
can't get you out of my head.
Don't care what is writ - ten in your
feels like it's deep with - in me.
Does - n't real - ly mat - ter if you're

F
G
C
his - to - ry
as long as you're here
with me.
on the run,
it seems like we're meant
to be.
I don't care who
Chorus:
F
C/E
Am
you are,
where you're from,
what you did,
as long
Gsus
G
F
1.
C/E
as you love me.
Who you are,
where you're from,
don't care what

2.
Am
Gsus
G
C
— you did, — as long — as you love — me.
— you're from, — don't care what —
F
C/E
Dm
G
F
— you did, — as long — as you love — me.
C/E
Am
Gsus
G
As long — as you love — me.

F
C/E
Am
As long
Esus
E7
Bridge:
Am
G
as you love me.
I've tried to hide it so that no one knows, but I guess
F
G
Am
it shows when you look in - to my eyes.
What you did and where you're
C/G
F♯m7(♭5)
F
G
com - ing from, I don't care,
as long as you love me, ba -

F
C
Am
Gsus
G
by.
I don't care who
Chorus:
F
C/E
Am
you are, where you're from, what you did, as long
Gsus
G
F
C/E
as you love me. Who you are, where you're from, don't care what
F
C/E
Dm
G
F
you did, as long as you love me. Who you are,

C/E
Am
Gsus
G
where_ you're from,_ what_ you did,_ as long_ as you love_
F
C/E
F
C/E
Dm
me. Who_ you are,_ where_ you're from,_ as long_
G
F
C/E
Dm
G
as you love_ me. Who_ you are,_ as long_ as you love_ me. What_
F
C/E
Dm
Gsus
G
C
you did,_ I don't care,_ as long_ as you love_ me._

. . . BABY ONE MORE TIME

Words and Music by
MAX MARTIN

G7/B
G7
E♭
Oh, ba - by, ba - by, I should - n't have let you go. And
Oh, pret - ty ba - by, there's noth - ing that I would - n't do. It's
Fm
G
Cm
Pre-chorus:
G7/B
G7
now you're out of sight, yeah.
not the way I planned it.
Show me how you want it to be. Tell me,
E♭
Fm
G
Cm
Chorus:
ba - by, 'cause I need to know now. Oh, be - cause my lone - li - ness is
G7/B
G7
E♭
Fm
Gsus
G
kill - ing me, and I, I must con - fess I still be - lieve (still be - lieve

Cm
G7/B
A♭
B♭
E♭
To Coda
__) that when I'm not with you I lose my mind. Give me a sign.__
1.
2.
Fm
G
Cm
N.C.
Hit me, ba - by, one more time.
Hit me, ba - by, one more time.
Oh, ba - by, ba - by.
Oh, ba - by, ba - by.
Bridge:
Oh, ba - by, ba - by, how was I sup - posed__ to know?__

Fm Gsus G A♭maj7 B♭

Oh, pretty baby, I should-n't have let you go.

Fm7 A♭ B♭ Cm

I must con-fess that my lone-li-ness

G7/B G7 E♭ Fm Gsus G

is kill-ing me now. Don't you know I still be-lieve

A♭ B♭ A♭maj7 E♭/G Fm *D.S. 𝄋 al Coda* N.C.

that you will be here and give me a sign. Hit me, ba-by, one more time.

Coda
Fm
G
Cm
G7/B
G7
Hit me, ba - by, one more time.
I must con - fess
that my lone - li - ness
is kill - ing me now.
E♭
Fm
Gsus
G
Cm
Don't you know I still be - lieve
that you will be here
G7/B
A♭
B♭
E♭
Fm
G
Cm
and give me a sign.
Hit me, ba - by, one more time.

From the Motion Picture AUSTIN POWERS: The Spy Who Shagged Me

BEAUTIFUL STRANGER

Words and Music by
MADONNA CICCONE and WILLIAM ORBIT

C#7sus
C#7
C#7sus
for me.
I've had the taste for dan - ger.
C#7
Verses 2 & 3:
C#7sus
C#7
2. If I'm smart, then I'll run a - way.
3. If I'm smart, then I'll run a - way.
C#7sus
C#7
C#7sus
But I'm not, so I'll guess I'll stay. Heav - en for - bid.
But I'm not, so I'll guess I'll stay. Have - n't you heard?
C#7
C#7sus
C#7
I'll take my chance on a beau - ti - ful strang - er.
I fell in love with a beau - ti - ful strang - er.

Bridge:
B
A
1. I looked in - to your eyes, and my world
2. I looked in - to your face, my heart was
3. I looked in - to your eyes, and my world
C♯7sus
C♯7
came tum - bl - ing down.
danc - in' all o - ver the place.
came tum - bl - ing down.
B
A
You're the dev - il in dis - guise. That's why I'm
I'd like to change my point of view, if I could
You're the dev - il in dis - guise. That's why I'm
C♯7sus
C♯7
sing - ing this song.
just for - get a - bout you.
sing - ing this song to you.

Chorus:
F♯
E
B
To know you is to love you.
C♯7sus
C♯7
C♯7sus
To Coda
You're ev - 'ry-where I go.
And ev - 'ry - bod - y
1.
C♯7
F♯
knows.
To love you
E
B
C♯7sus
is to be part of you.
I paid for you with

C♯7
C♯7sus
C♯7
tears
and swal-lowed all my pride.
E
B
F♯
A
C♯7sus
Da da da da da da da da da da da da da.
Beau - ti - ful
C♯7
E
B
F♯
A
strang - er.
Da da da da da da da da da da da da da.
C♯7
C♯7sus
Beau - ti - ful strang - er.

2.
D.S. 𝄋 al Coda
C♯7
knows.
𝄌 Coda
C♯7sus
I paid for you with
tears
and swal-lowed all my pride.
E
B
F♯
A
Da da da da da da da da da da da da da.
Beau - ti - ful

C♯7
E
B
F♯
A
strang - er.
Da da da da da da da da da da da da da.
C♯7
C♯7sus
Beau - ti - ful strang - er.
C♯7
C♯7sus
C♯7
Repeat ad lib. and fade

BAILAMOS

Words and Music by
PAUL BARRY and MARK TAYLOR

Dm7
We take the floor,
Now, I'm let - ting go,
G
F
E
noth - ing is for - bid - den an - y - more.
there is some - thing I think you should know.
Don't let the
I won't be
Am
F
world in out - side;
don't let a mo - ment go by.
leav - ing your side;
we're gon - na dance through the night.
C
G
E
Noth - ing can stop us to - night.
I wan - na reach for the stars.
Bai - la -

Chorus:
Am
G
F
mos,
let the rhy-thm take_ you o - ver, bai - la - mos._
Am
G
F
_
Te quie - ro, a-mor mi-o, bai - la -
Am
G
F
mos.
Wan-na live this night_ for - ev - er, bai - la - mos._
Am
G
F
_
Te quie - ro, a-mor mi-o, te quie-

1. E
Am
ro.
Dm
Am
Dm
2. E
Bridge:
Am
ro.
Whoa,
to -
G
F
Am
G
F
night we dance, whoa, like no to - mor - row.

Am
G
F
Am
Whoa, if you will stay with me.
E
Am
G
F
(whispered:) Te quiero, mi amor.
Am
G
F
Am
G
F
Am
G
F
Bai-la -

Chorus:
Am
G
F
mos,
let the rhy-thm take you o - ver, bai - la - mos.
Te quie - ro, a - mor mi - o, bai - la -
mos.
Wan-na live this night for - ev - er, bai - la - mos.
Repeat ad lib. and fade
Te quie - ro, a - mor mi - o, bai - la -

BECAUSE OF YOU

Words and Music by
ANDERS BAGGE, ARNTHOR BIRGISSON,
CHRISTIAN KARLSSON and PATRICK TUCKER

Verse:

C G/B Dm7 C G/B

1. Ba - by, I real - ly know by now, since we met___ that day, you showed me

2. *See additional lyrics*

Dm7 Am7 C/G F C/E

the way. I failed you, then you gave me love. I can't de - scribe how much__

Dm7 G F/A G7/B C G/B

__ I feel__ for you.____ I said, ba - by, I should have known

Dm7 C G/B Dm7

by now. Should have been right there when - ev - er you gave me love. And if

Am7
C/G
F
C/E
Dm7
on - ly you were here,
I'd tell you, yes, I'd tell
G
F/A
G7/B
Chorus:
C
G/B
Dm7
you. You're my sun - shine af - ter the rain. You're my
C
G/B
Dm7
Am7
C/G
cure a - gainst my fear and my pain. 'Cause I'm los - ing my mind when you're
1.
F
C/E
Dm7
G
F/A
G7/B
not a - round. It's all, it's all, it's all be - cause of you.

C
G/B
Dm7
C
G/B
Dm7
2.
Bridge:
F/A
G7/B
B♭
F
be - cause of you. If I knew how to tell you what's on
Em7
A7
G/B
A7/C♯
Dm
C
my mind. Then I'd al - ways be there,
(Make you un - der - stand.
B♭
F
G
F/A
G7/B
right by your side. You're my
)

Verse 2:
Honestly, could it be you and me
Like it was before, need less or more?
'Cause when I close my eyes
At night, I realize that no one else
Could ever take your place.
I still can feel, and it's so real,
When you're touching me,
Kisses endlessly.
It's just a place in the sun
Where our love's begun.
I miss you, yes, I miss you.
(To Chorus:)

BELIEVE

Words and Music by
BRIAN HIGGINS, STUART McLENNAN,
PAUL BARRY, STEPHEN TORCH,
MATT GRAY and TIM POWELL

* Original recording in G♭ major.

C
F
talk-ing to you.
turn - ing back.
It's so sad that you're leav -
I need time to move
Am
Bb
- ing, takes time to be-lieve it,
on I need love to feel strong,
but af-ter all is
'cause I've had time to
C
said and done,
think it through,
you're going to be the lone - ly one, oh.
and may-be I'm too good for you, oh.
F
C
Gm
3fr
Bb
Do you be - lieve in life af-ter love?
I can feel

F
C
Gm
3fr
Dm
some-thing in-side me say, I real-ly don't think you're strong e - nough, no.
Chorus:
F
C
Gm
3fr
B♭
Do you be - lieve in life af-ter love? I can feel
F
C
Gm
3fr
Dm
some-thing in-side me say, I real-ly don't think you're strong e - nough, no.
Bridge:
Dm
C
But I know that I'll get through this,

Dm
'cause I know that I am strong.
C
Bb
I don't need you a-ny-more,
I don't need
C
Bb
you a-ny-more,
Oh, I don't need you a-ny-more,
Gm7
3fr
C
no, I don't need you a-ny-more.

Chorus:
F
C
Gm
3fr
B♭
Do you be - lieve in life af - ter love?
I can feel
something in - side me say,
I real-ly don't think you're strong e - nough, no.
Am7
Dm
Repeat ad lib. and fade

BETTER DAYS

Words and Music by
BRUCE SPRINGSTEEN

Bm
-row to come, or that train to come roar-in' 'round the bend. I got a
Em
new suit of clothes, a pret-ty red rose and a wom-an I can call my friend.
Chorus:
G
D
These are bet-ter days, ba - by.
Yeah, there's bet-ter
These are
days shin - ing through.
bet - ter days, it's true.
G
D
These are bet-ter days, ba - by,
1.
D.S. 𝄋
Em
G
D
A
bet - ter days with a girl like you.
There's (2nd time only)
2. Well,

Verse 2:
Well, I took a piss at fortune's sweet kiss,
It's like eating caviar and dirt.
It's a sad, funny ending to find yourself pretending
A rich man in a poor man's shirt.
Now, my ass was draggin' when from a passin' gypsy wagon,
Your heart, like a diamond shone.
Tonight I'm layin' in your arms, carvin' lucky charms
Out of these hard luck bones.

Chorus 2:
These are better days, baby.
These are better days, it's true.
These are better days.
There's better days shining through.

Verse 3:
Now, a life of leisure and a pirate's treasure
Don't make much for tragedy.
But it's a sad man, my friend, who's livin' in his own skin
And can't stand the company.
Every fool's got a reason for feelin' sorry for himself
And turning his heart to stone.
Tonight, this fool's halfway to heaven and just a mile outta hell,
And I feel like I'm comin' home.
(To Chorus:)

(YOU DRIVE ME) CRAZY

Words and Music by JÖRGEN ELOFSSON,
DAVID KREUGER, PER MAGNUSSON and MAX MARTIN

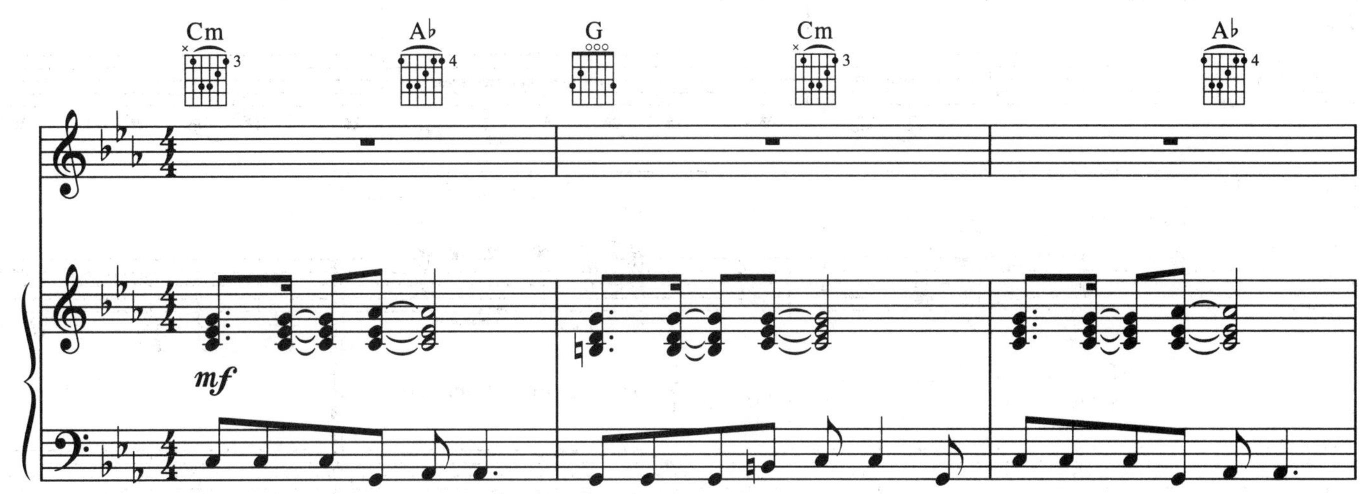

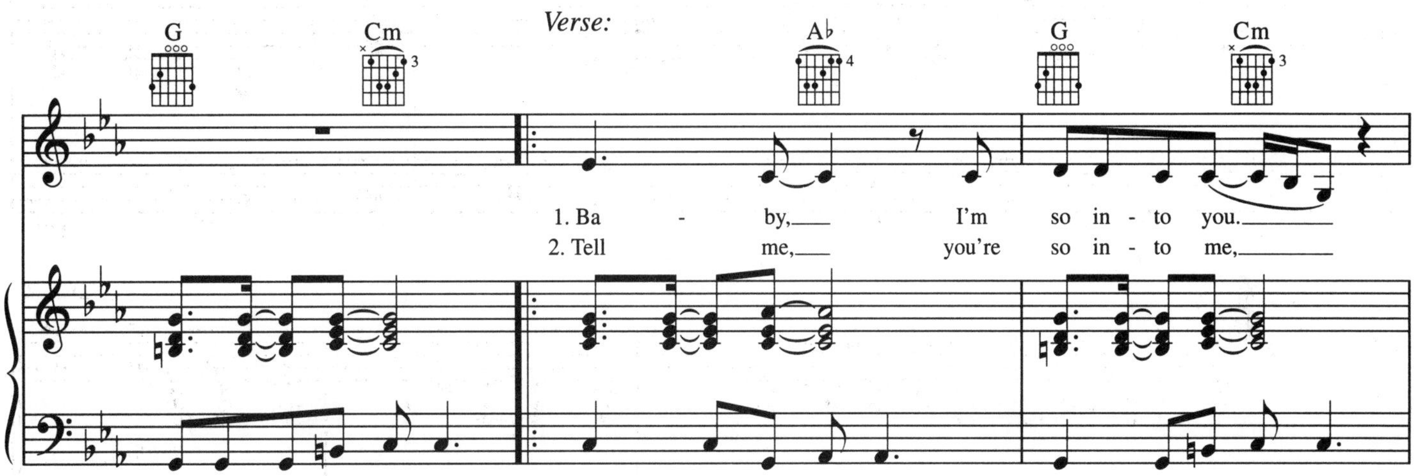

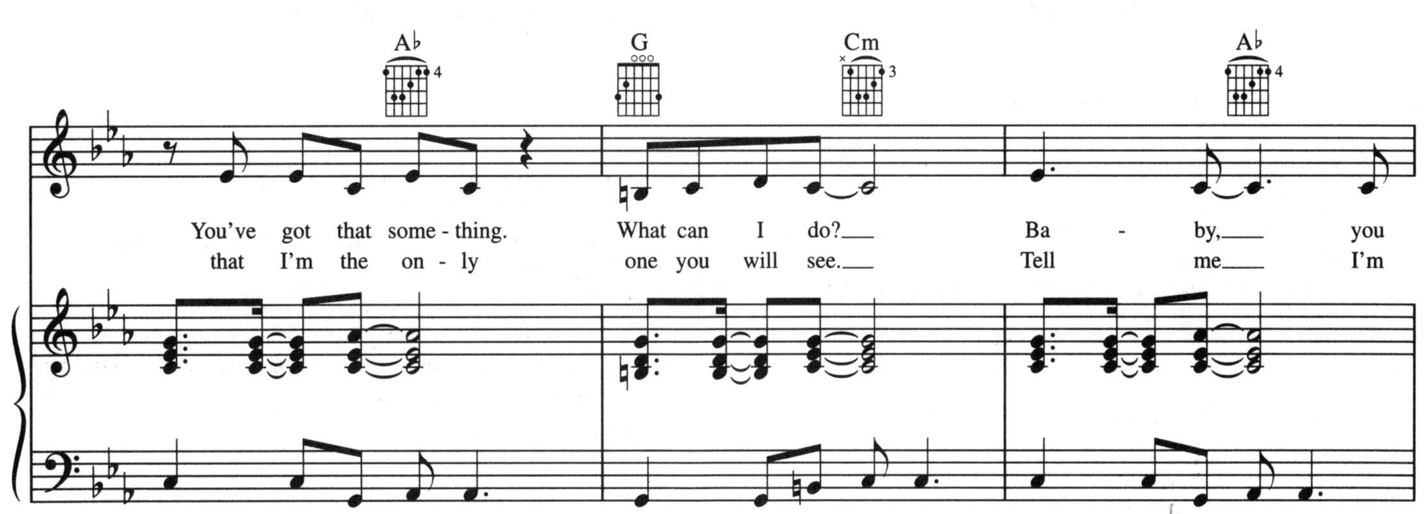

G
Cm
A♭
G
Cm
spin me a - round.
not in the blue,
The earth is mov - ing,
that I'm not wast - ing
but I
my
can't feel the ground.
feel - ings on you.
1st time only
A♭
G
Cm
A♭
Ev - 'ry time you look at me,
my heart is jump - ing. It's
G
Cm
A♭
G
Cm
eas - y to see.
Lov - in' you means so much more,
A♭
G
Cm
Chorus:
A♭
more than an - y - thing I ev - er felt be - fore. You drive me cra - zy, I

G Cm Ab G Cm

just can't sleep. I'm so ex-cit-ed, I'm in too deep. You drive me

Ab Bb Eb Bb/D Cm Ab

cra-zy, but it feels al-right. Ba-by, think-in' of you keeps me

1. G Cm Ab G Cm

up all night.

Ab G Cm 2. G Cm

up all night.

Bridge:
E♭
Cra - zy, I just can't sleep. I'm so ex-cit-ed, I'm
C♭maj7
B♭m7
E♭m7
in too deep. Cra - zy, but it feels al - right.
C♭
B♭7sus
B♭7
Cm
A♭
Ev - 'ry day and ev - 'ry night.
G
Cm
A♭
G
Cm
You drive me

A♭ G Cm A♭

cra - zy, I'm so ex - cit - ed, I'm
You drive me cra - zy, ba - by.

G Cm A♭ B♭ E♭ B♭/D

in too deep. Oh, cra - zy, but it feels al - right.

Cm A♭ 1. G Cm 2. G Cm

Ba - by, think - in' of you keeps me up all night. You drive me up all night.

A♭ Fm7 G Cm

Ba - by, think - in' of you keeps me up all night.

COUNT ON ME

Words and Music by
BABYFACE, WHITNEY HOUSTON
and MICHAEL HOUSTON

Em7
F♯
Bm
Em11
7fr
D/F♯
Don't be a - fraid.
Please be - lieve me when I say,
Em9/A
Dmaj7
Em7
count on.
I can see it's hurt - ing you.
Dmaj7/F♯
Em7
Dmaj7
Em7
I can feel your pain.
It's hard to see the sun - shine through the
Am9
5fr
D7
Gmaj9
A7/G
rain.
I know some-times it seems as if it's

F♯m7
Bm7
2fr
Em7
nev - er gon - na end, but you'll get through it, just
Em9/A
Chorus:
D
Em7
don't give in. 'Cause you can count on me through thick and thin, a friend -
D/F♯
Gmaj13
3fr
D/A
A/G
- ship that will nev - er end. When you are weak, I will be strong,
D(9)/F♯
G(9)
Dmaj7/F♯
Bm
help - ing you to car - ry on. Call on me, I will be there.

Em7
F♯
Bm
Em11
7 fr
D/F♯
To Coda I
To Coda II
Don't be a - fraid.
Please be - lieve me when I say,
Em7/A
D
Em7
count on, you can count on me.
Ah,
D/F♯
Em7
D
Em7
Am7
D7
yes you can.
I know
Bridge:
Gmaj9
A/G
F♯m7
Bm
some - times it seems as if we're stand-in' all a - lone.
But

Em7
Em7/A
D.S. 𝄋 al Coda I
we'll get through it, 'cause love won't let us fold.
Coda I
Em9/A
G/B
F♯7/C♯
count on. There's a place in - side of all of us where our
Bm/D
B7/D♯
Em
F♯7
faith in love be - gins. You should reach to find the truth in love, the
Bm
Em7
A/G
an - swer's there with - in. I know that life can make you feel it's much

F♯m7
Bm
Em7
Em7/A
D.S. 𝄋 al Coda II
hard-er than _ it real-ly is, ___ but we'll get through it, just don't, don't give _ in.
Coda II
F♯m/A Em7/A
count on, count on, count on, count on, count on, count on, count on
Dmaj7
Em7
Dmaj7
Em7
me. ___ Ah, yes you can, _
Dmaj7
Em7
Dmaj7
know I can, oh yeah. _ count on me. __
__ sure you can, So glad I can _ count on me, __

DO I HAVE TO SAY THE WORDS?

Lyrics and Music by
BRYAN ADAMS, JIM VALLANCE
and R.J. LANGE

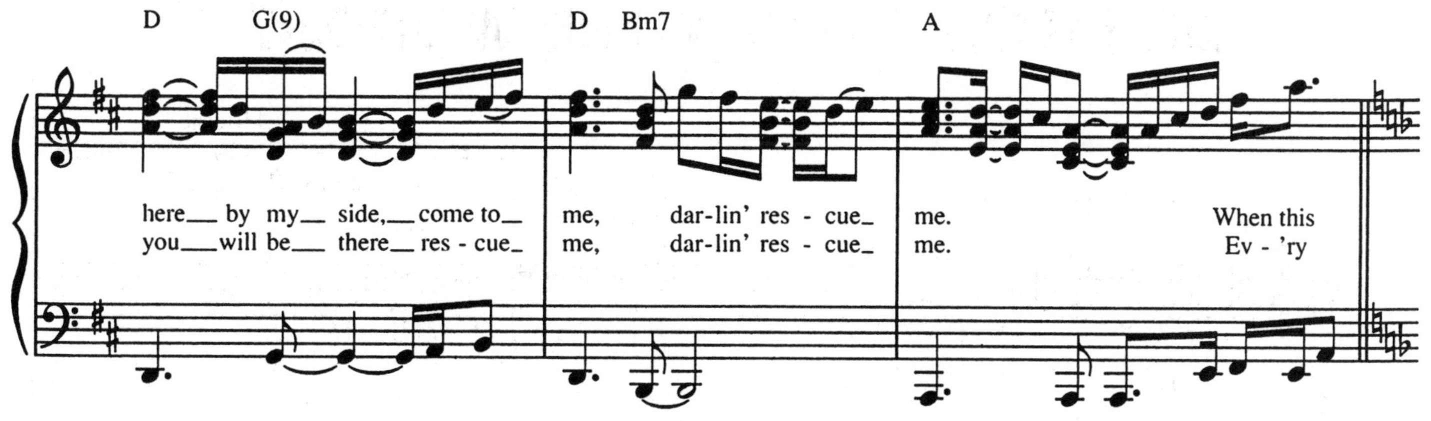
D
G(9)
D
Bm7
A
here__ by my__ side,__ come to__
you__ will be__ there__ res - cue__
me, dar-lin' res - cue__
me, dar-lin' res - cue__
me.
me.
When this
Ev - 'ry

F
B♭maj7
F
B♭maj7
world's__ clos - ing__ in__ there's no__
dream__ that we__ share,__ ev - 'ry__
need__ to pre - tend,__ set me__
cross__ that we__ bear,__ come to__

Dm
Gm7
Csus
C
free, dar - lin' res - cue__
me, dar - lin' res - cue__
me,
me,
oh.__

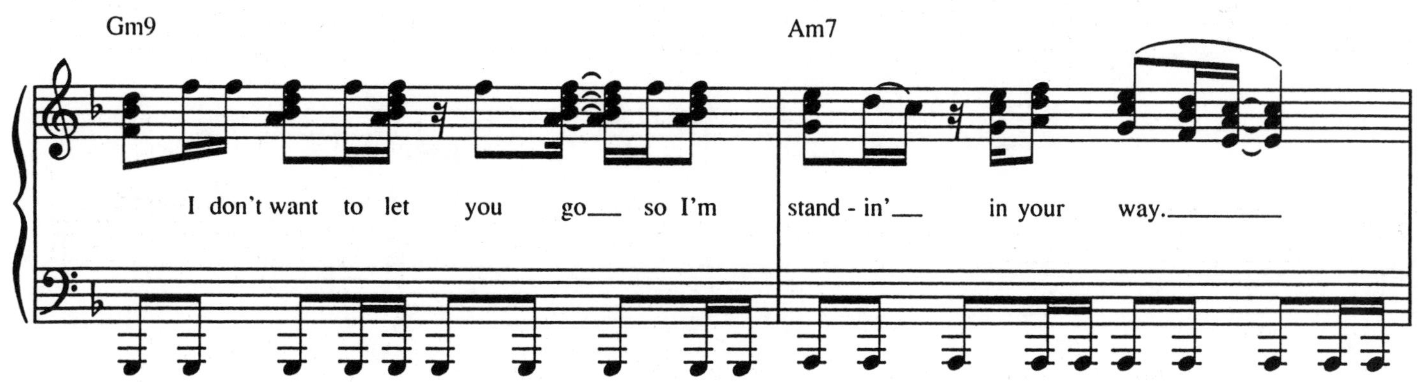
Gm9
Am7
I don't want to let you go__ so I'm
stand - in'__ in your way.__

B♭
C
I nev - er need - ed an - y - one__ like I'm need - in' you__ to - day. Do I
N.C.
Chorus:
Dm
Gm
have to say the words?
Do I have to tell the truth?
C
F
B♭
Do I have to shout__ it out?__
Gm
C
Dm
Do I have to say a prayer?
Must I prove__ to you__
B♭
To Coda
C
how good we are__ to - geth - er?
Do I have to say the words?

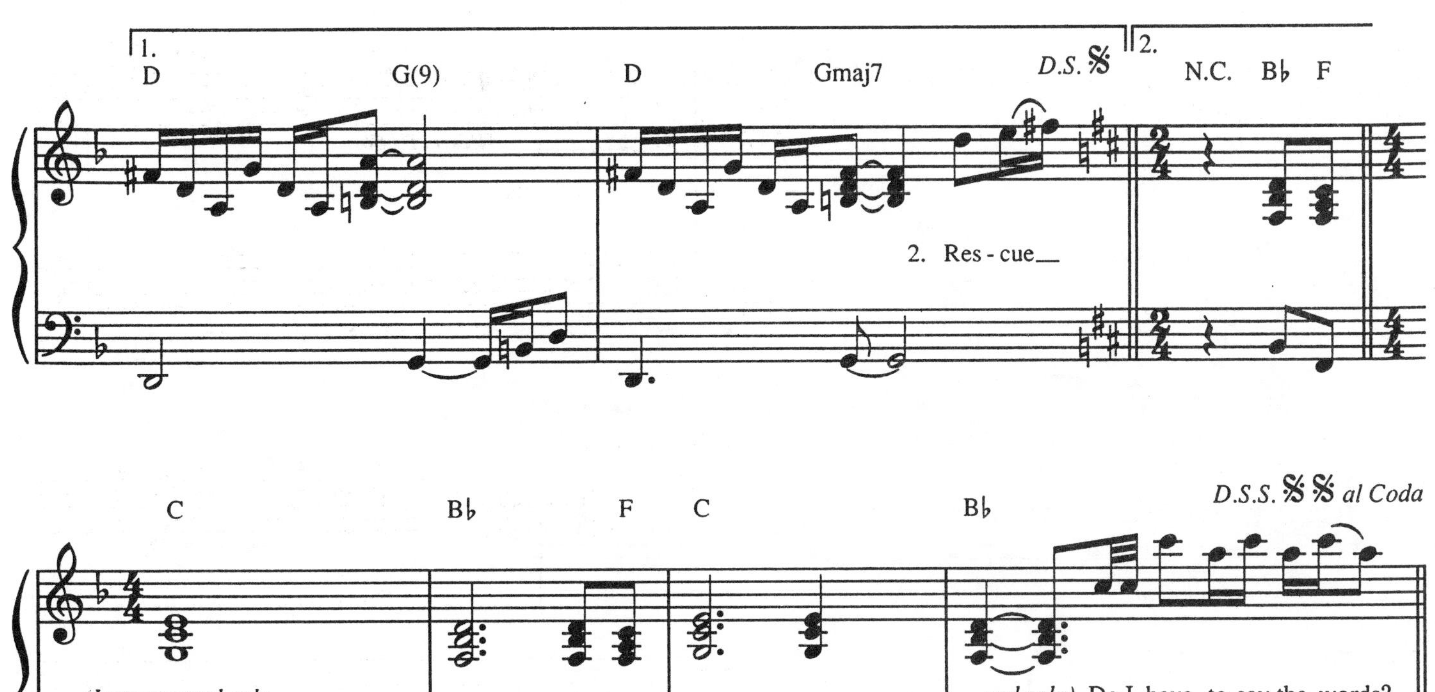
1.
D
G(9)
D
Gmaj7
D.S. 𝄋
2.
N.C. B♭ F
2. Res - cue

C
B♭
F
C
B♭
D.S.S. 𝄋𝄋 al Coda
(Instrumental solo . . .
. . . end solo) Do I have to say the words?
𝄌 Coda
C
N.C.
D
G(9)
- er?
Do I have to say the words?
(Ad lib. vocals)
(Instrumental solo 3rd time to end)

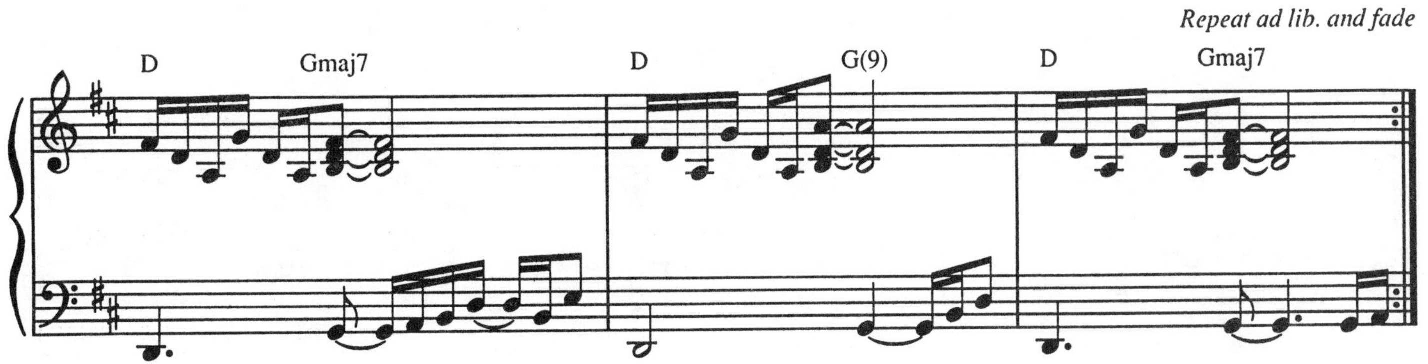
Repeat ad lib. and fade
D
Gmaj7
D
G(9)
D
Gmaj7

DOWN SO LONG

Words and Music by
JEWEL KILCHER

Am G F G

My pock - et - book and my heart both just got sto - len, and that

Am G F G

sun act like she don't e - ven care.

Verses 2 & 3:

Am G F G

2. The wind blows cold when you reach the top. It feels like

3. *See additional lyrics*

Am G F G

some - one's face is stuck to the bot - tom of my shoe. I got a,

Am
G
F
G
a plas-tic Je-sus and cord-less tel-e-phone for ev-'ry cor-ner of my room. Got
Am
G
F
ev-'ry-bod-y but you tell-ing me what to do.
Chorus:
G
F
C
G/B
Am
G
But I've been down so long,
F
C
G/B
Am
G
F
ooh, it can't be long-er still. I've been down so

To Coda
1.
C
G/B
Am
G
F
G
Am
G
long that the end must be draw - ing near.
F
G
Am
G
F
G
2.
F
G
Am
G
F
G
end must be draw - ing near, ee oh ee oh.
Oh ee oh ee oh.
Am
G
F
G
Oh ee oh ee oh, oh.

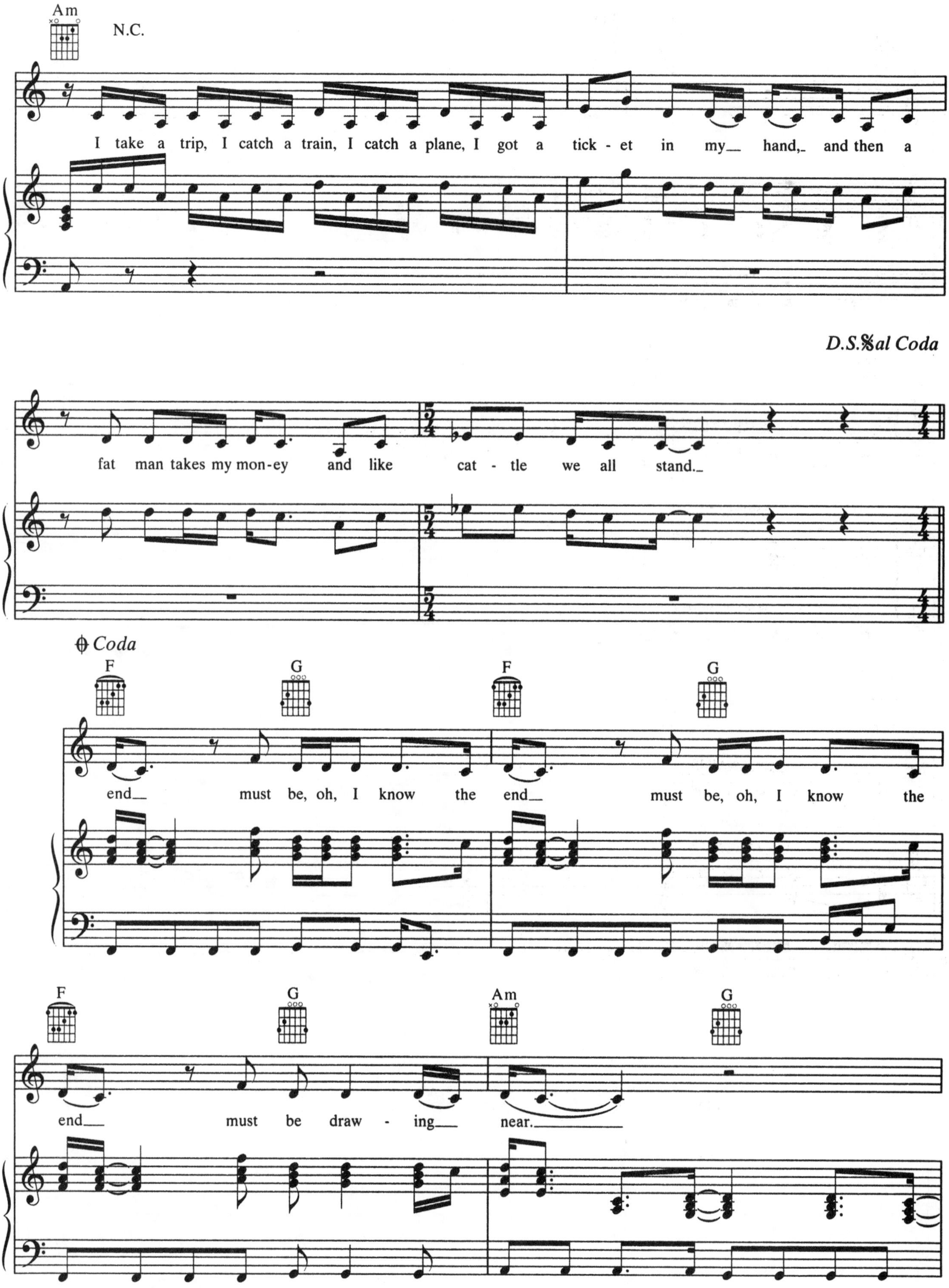

D.S. 𝄋 al Coda

fat man takes my mon-ey and like cat - tle we all stand._

𝄌 *Coda*

F G F G

end__ must be, oh, I know the end__ must be, oh, I know the

F G Am G

end__ must be draw - ing__ near.______

Verse 3:
I look to everybody but me to answer my prayers,
Till I saw an angel in a bathroom who said she saw no one worth saving anywhere.
And a blind man on the corner said it's simple, like flipping a coin:
Don't matter what side it lands on if it's someone else's dime.
(To Chorus:)

From the LUCASFILM LTD. Production **"STAR WARS: Episode I** ***The Phantom Menace*****"**

DUEL OF THE FATES

By
JOHN WILLIAMS

Maestoso, with great force

Allegro ♩ = 152

mf

mf
Kor - ah,
Rah - tah - mah.
mf
3
3
3

Yood - hah,
Kor - ah.
f

f
Kor - ah,
Syahd - ho.
Rah - tah - mah,
Daan - yah.
Kor - ah,

Kee - lah,
Daan - yah.
Nyo - hah,
Kee - lah,
Kor - ah,
Rah-tah-mah.
Syahd - ho,
Kee - lah,
Kor - ah,
Rah-tah-mah.
ff
Kor - ah,
ff
ff

Daan - yah.
Kor - ah,
Rah - tah - mah.
mf
cresc. poco a poco
f
ff
p

p
3
Kor - ah,
Daan - yah.
p
3
3
3
mf
3
Kor - ah,
Rah - tah - mah.
mf
3
3
3
mf

ff
Nyo-ha, Kee-lah, Kor - ah, Rah - tah - ma. Syahd-ho, Kee-lah,
Daan-ya, Rah-tah-ma. Kor - ah!
mf
f
ff

from WAITING TO EXHALE

EXHALE
(Shoop Shoop)

Words and Music by
BABYFACE

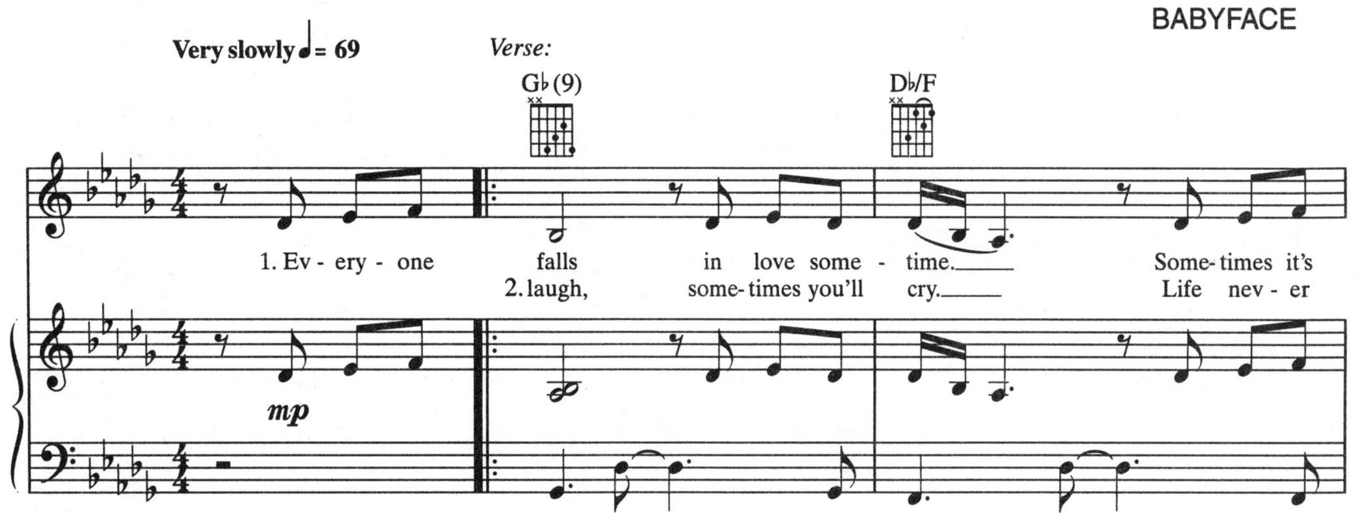

Exhale - 5 - 1

Chorus:
G♭maj7
D♭/F
shoop, shoop, shoop, shoo be doop. Shoop, shoop, shoo be
E♭m7
D♭
doop. Shoop, shoop, shoo be
doop. Shoop, shoop, shoo be
All you got - ta do is say shoo be
G♭
D♭/F
doop. Shoop, shoop, shoo be doop. Shoop, shoop, shoo be
E♭m7
1. D♭
2. D♭
doop. Shoop, shoop, shoo be doop. 2. Some - times you'll doop.

Bridge:
F7sus
F7/A
Hearts are of - ten bro - ken when there are words un - spo - ken.
B♭m
B♭m/A♭
In your soul there's an - swers to your prayers. If you're
E♭m7
D♭/F
search - ing for a place you know, a fa - mil - iar face, some - where to go, you should
G♭(9)
E♭m7/A♭
look in - side your - self, you're half - way there.
2. Some - times you'll

laugh, some - times you'll cry. Life nev - er
tells us the when's or why's. But when you've got
friends to wish you well, you'll find your
point when you will ex - hale, yeah, yeah. Say,

Chorus:

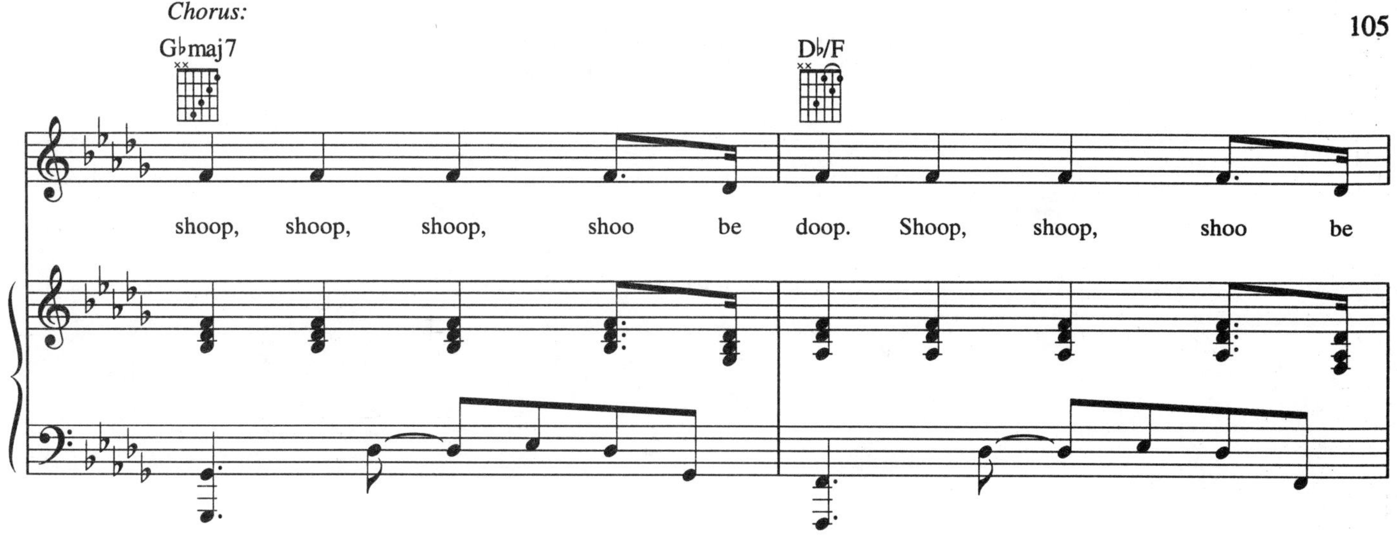

G♭maj7
D♭/F
shoop, shoop, shoop, shoo be doop. Shoop, shoop, shoo be

E♭m7
D♭
G♭
doop. Shoop, shoop, shoo be doop. Shoop, shoop, shoo be doop. Shoop, shoop, shoo be

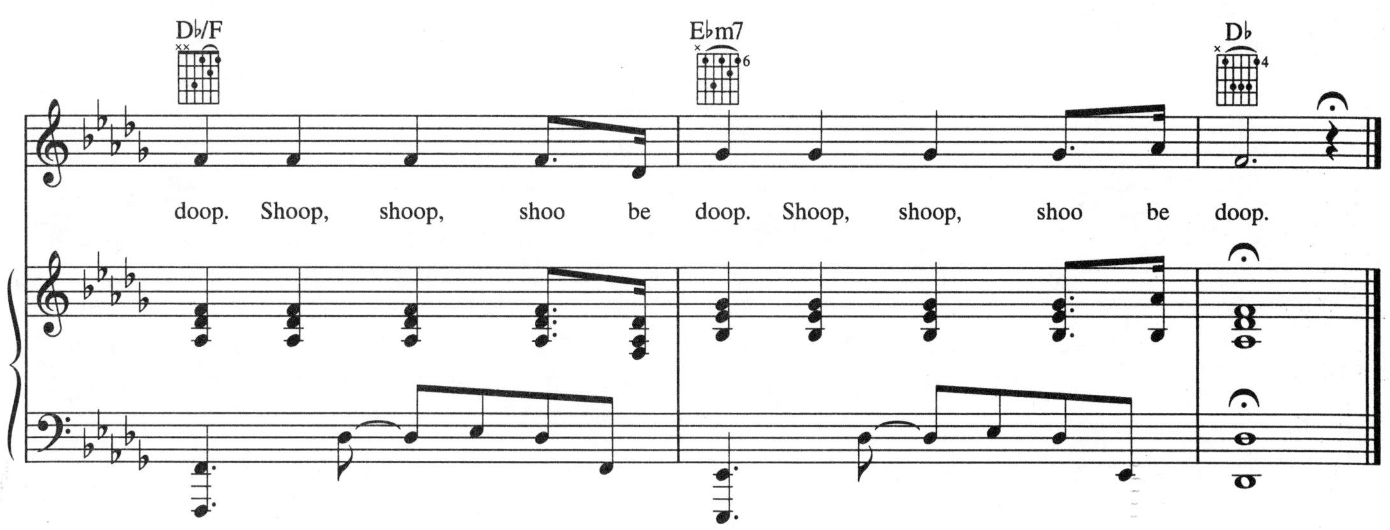

D♭/F
E♭m7
D♭
doop. Shoop, shoop, shoo be doop. Shoop, shoop, shoo be doop.

FOOLISH GAMES

Words and Music by
JEWEL KILCHER

Moderately slow ♩ = 66

Dm Bb

mp

(with pedal)

F C

Verse:

Dm Bb

1. You took your coat off and stood in the
2.3.4. *See additional lyrics*

F C

rain, you're al-ways cra - zy like that.

Dm Bb

And I watched from my win - dow, al-ways felt I was

* *Vocal sung one octave lower*

F
C
1.3.
2.4.
out - side_ look-ing_ in_ on you.
Pre-Chorus:
Gm
B♭
1. In case_ you failed to no-tice, in case you failed to see,
2. See additional lyrics
F
C
this is_ my heart_ bleed - ing_ be - fore you, this is me down_ on_ my_ knees.
Chorus:
B♭
C
F
C/E
These_ fool-ish games_ are_ tear - ing_ me_ a-part,
Dm
B♭
C
and your_ thought-less words_

Verse 2:
You're always the mysterious one with
Dark eyes and careless hair,
You were fashionably sensitive
But too cool to care.
You stood in my doorway with nothing to say
Besides some comment on the weather.
(To Pre-Chorus:)

Verse 3:
You're always brilliant in the morning,
Smoking your cigarettes and talking over coffee.
Your philosophies on art, Baroque moved you.
You loved Mozart and you'd speak of your loved ones
As I clumsily strummed my guitar.

Verse 4:
You'd teach me of honest things,
Things that were daring, things that were clean.
Things that knew what an honest dollar did mean.
I hid my soiled hands behind my back.
Somewhere along the line, I must have gone
Off track with you.

Pre-Chorus 2:
Excuse me, think I've mistaken you for somebody else,
Somebody who gave a damn, somebody more like myself.
(To Chorus:)

FOR YOU I WILL

Words and Music by
DIANE WARREN

Cm7
Cm7/F
B♭
F/A
I will be there. Any time the times get too tough, any time your
won't let you down. If there is a mountain to move, I will move that
Gm7
F/G
Gm7
Cm7
Dm7
best ain't enough, I'll be the one to make it better.
mountain for you. I'm here for you, I'm here forever.
A♭maj7
Gm7
Cm7
I'll be there to protect you, see you through.
I will be a fortress, tall and strong. I'll
E♭m7
Cm7
Cm7/F
I'll be there, and there is nothing I won't do.
keep you safe, I'll stand beside you, right or wrong.
I will cross the

Chorus:
B♭
F/A
Gm7
Dm7
Cm7
Cm7/F
o - cean for you, I will go and bring you the moon, I will be your he - ro, your strength, an - y - thing
you need. I will be the sun in your sky, I will light your way for all time, prom - ise you,
To Coda
1.
E♭m7
E♭/F
for you, I will.
2. I will shield your
2.
Bridge:
A♭maj7
E♭/G
For you, I will lay my life on the line.

D7/F♯
Gm7
For you, I'll fight, for you, I will die. With ev-
Cm7
B♭/D
D7/F♯
Gm7
-ery breath, with all my soul, I give my word, I'll give it all.
E♭m7
Cm7/F
D.S. 𝄋 al Coda
Put your faith in me, I'll do an-y-thing. I will cross the
𝄌 Coda
B♭
F/A
Cm7/F
Dm7/G
I will, I will, I will.
I will cross the

Chorus:

C G/B Am7 Em7 Dm7 Dm7/G

o-cean for you, I will go and bring you the moon, I will be your he-ro, your strength, an-y-thing

C Dm7/G C G/B Am7 Em7

you need. I will be the sun in your sky, I will light your way for all time, prom-ise you,

Dm7 Dm7/G C Dm7 Dm7/G

for you, I will. Prom-ise you, for you, I will.

C Dm7 Dm7/G *Freely* C

I prom-ise you, for you, I will.

rit.

FROZEN

Words and Music by
MADONNA CICCONE and
PATRICK LEONARD

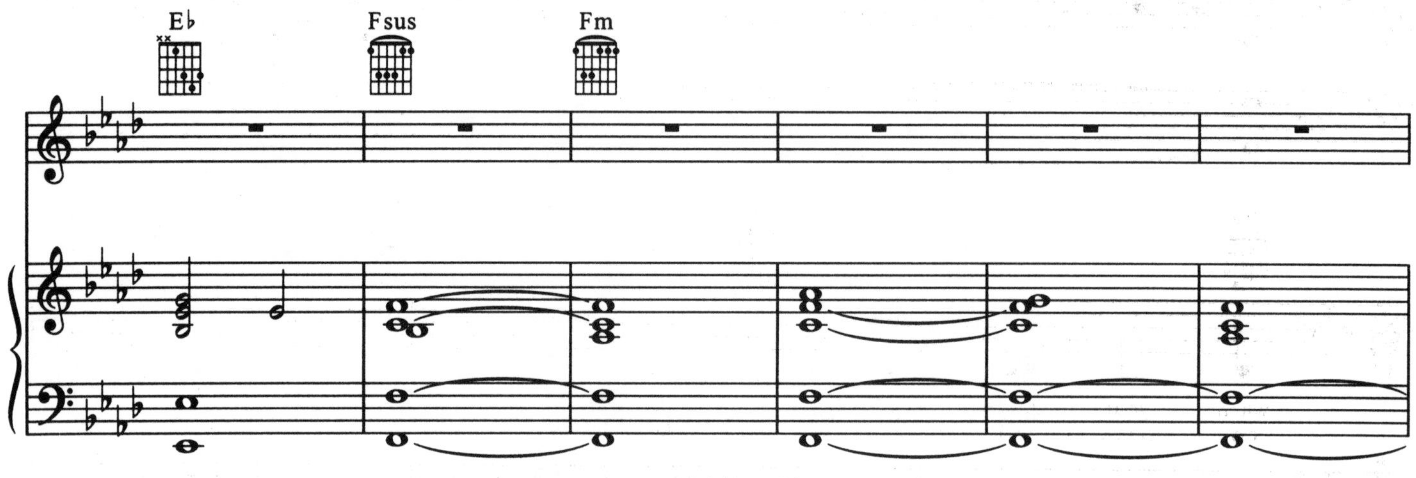

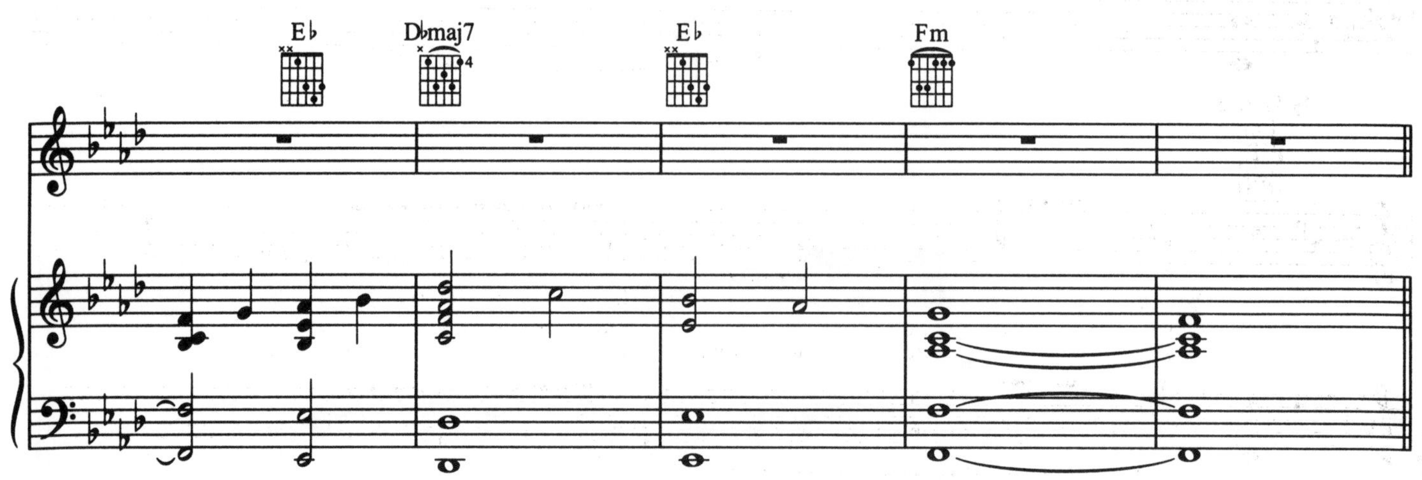

Verses 1 & 2:

Fm

1. You on - ly see what your eyes want to see.
2. Now, there's no point in plac - ing the blame,

Eb/F Db

How can life be what you want it to be?___ You're fro - zen
and How should know I suf - fer the same.___ If I should lose___ you,

Eb Fm Eb/F

when your heart's not o - pen.
my heart will be bro - ken.

𝄋 *Verse 3:*

Fm

You're so con - sumed with how much you get.___
Love is a bird, she needs to fly.___
3. You on - ly see what your eyes want to see.___

E♭/F
D♭
You waste your time with hate and re - gret.___ You're bro - ken
Let all the hurt in - side of you die.___ You're fro - zen
How can life be what you want it to be?___ You're fro - zen
E♭
Fm
E♭/F
Fm
when your heart's not o - pen.
when your heart's not o - pen.
when your heart's not o - pen.
Chorus:
Fm
B♭m
D♭
A♭
Mm,___ if I could melt your___ heart,
Fm
B♭m
G♭
A♭sus
mm,___ we'd nev - er be a - part.

Fm
B♭m
D♭
A♭
Mm, give your-self to me.
Fm
B♭m
G♭
A♭sus
To Coda
Mm, you hold
Fm
the key.
1.
2.
N.C.

1.
2.
D.S. al Coda
Coda
Fm
B♭m
D♭
A♭
the key.
If I could melt your heart.
Fm
B♭m
G♭
A♭
Fm
B♭m
G♭
A♭
Fm

HOUSE OF LOVE

Words and Music by
GREG BARNHILL, KENNY GREENBERG
and WALLY WILSON

D♭
Fm7
G♭maj7
bout it, some-times life is fun - ny. You think you're in your dark - est hour when the
Amaj7
B
D♭
D♭maj7
Fm7
lights are com-in' on in the house of love.
Verse:
G♭maj7
A♭
B♭m
Oh! 1. You've been up all night
A♭
B♭m
A♭
think-in' it was o - ver. He's been out of sight, at least for the mo-ment.

Gbmaj7
Ab
But when some-thing this strong, ooh, gets a hold on you, the odds are
Ebm7
Gbmaj7/Ab
To Coda
nine - ty - nine to one it's got a hold on him, too.
Chorus:
Db
Fm7
Well, I bet you an - y a - mount of mon - ey he'll be com - in'
Gbmaj7
B9
back to you. Ooh, I know there ain't no doubt a -

D♭
Fm7
G♭maj7
bout it, some-times life is fun - ny. You think you're in your dark - est hour when the
Amaj7
B
D♭
lights are com - in' on in the house of love. When the
1.
D.S. 𝄋
2.
D.S. 𝄋 al Coda
lights are com-in' on in the house of love. of love.
𝄌 Coda
Chorus:
E♭
Gm7
Well, I bet you an-y a-mount of mon-ey he'll be com-in'

A♭maj7 D♭9

back to you. Ooh, I know there ain't no doubt a -

E♭ Gm7

bout it, some - times life is fun - ny. You think you're in your

A♭maj7 C♭maj7 D♭

dark - est hour when the lights are com - in' on. Well, I

Verse 2:
Now, when the house is dark and you're all alone inside,
You've gotta listen to your heart, put away your foolish pride.
Though the storm is breakin' and thunder shakes the walls,
There with a firm foundation ain't it never, never, never gonna fall.
(To Chorus:)

Verse 3:
Though the storm is breakin' and thunder shakes the walls,
There with a firm foundation ain't it never, never, never gonna fall.
(To Chorus:)

HOW 'BOUT US

Words and Music by
DANA WALDEN

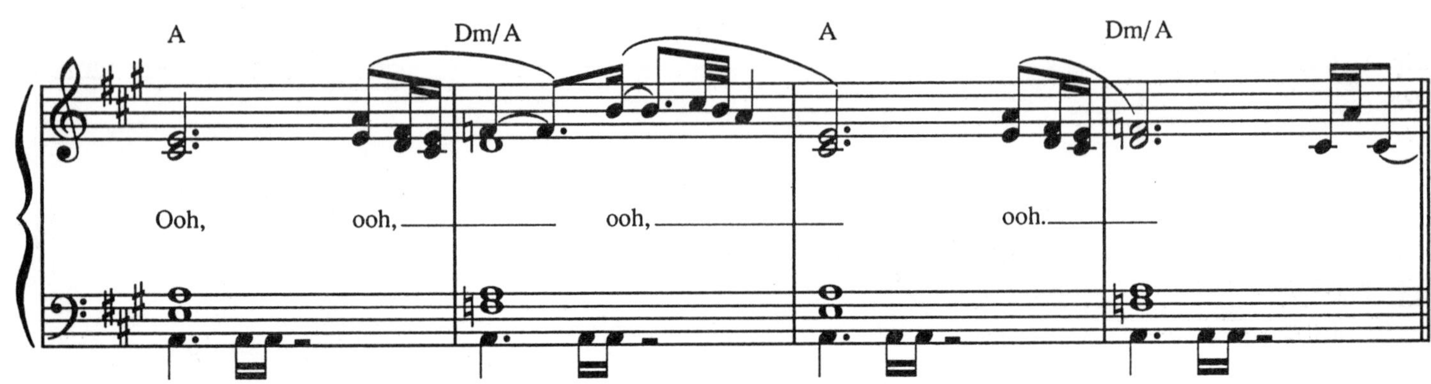

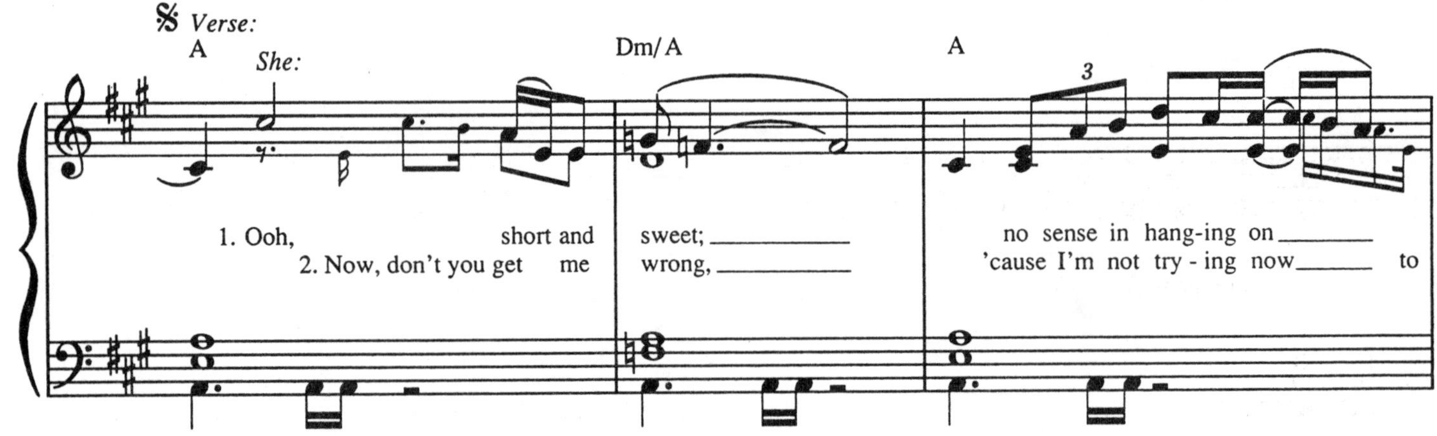

A
1.
Dm/A
and if the fi - re's out we should both be gone.
too man - y lov - er's hearts
G9
Both:
To Next Strain
2.
Dm/A
Oh.
lose their dream. (We won't lose it!)
cresc.
Chorus:
A
Both:
D/A
Some peo-ple are made for each oth - er;
some peo-ple can love one an-oth-er for life;
Dm/A
A
how 'bout us?

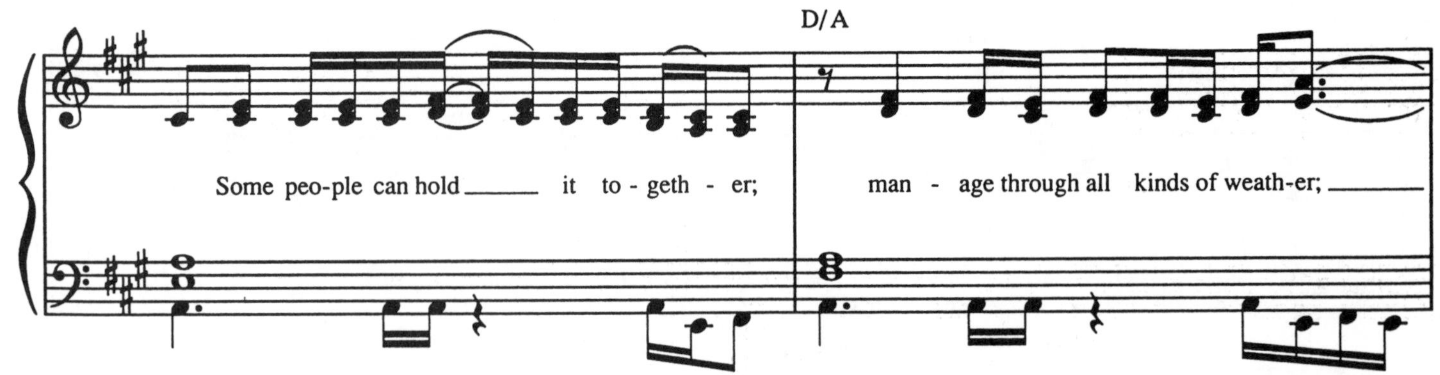
D/A
Some peo-ple can hold it to-geth - er;
man - age through all kinds of weath-er;

Dm/A
1.
A
Dm/A
Dm6/A
can
we?

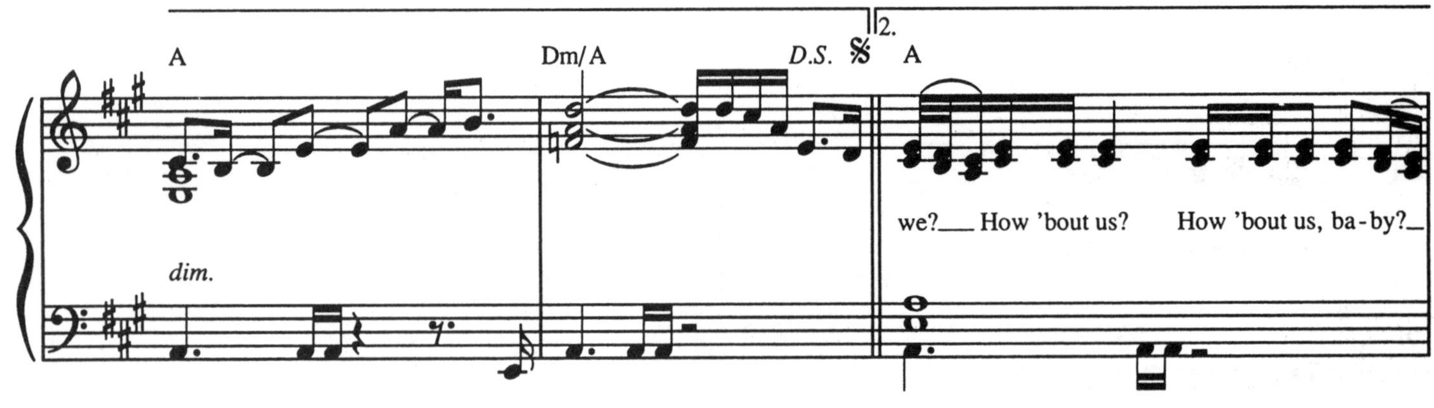
A
Dm/A
D.S.
2.
A
we? How 'bout us? How 'bout us, ba-by?
dim.

Dm6/A
A
How 'bout us? How 'bout us, ba - by?
How 'bout us? How 'bout us, ba - by?

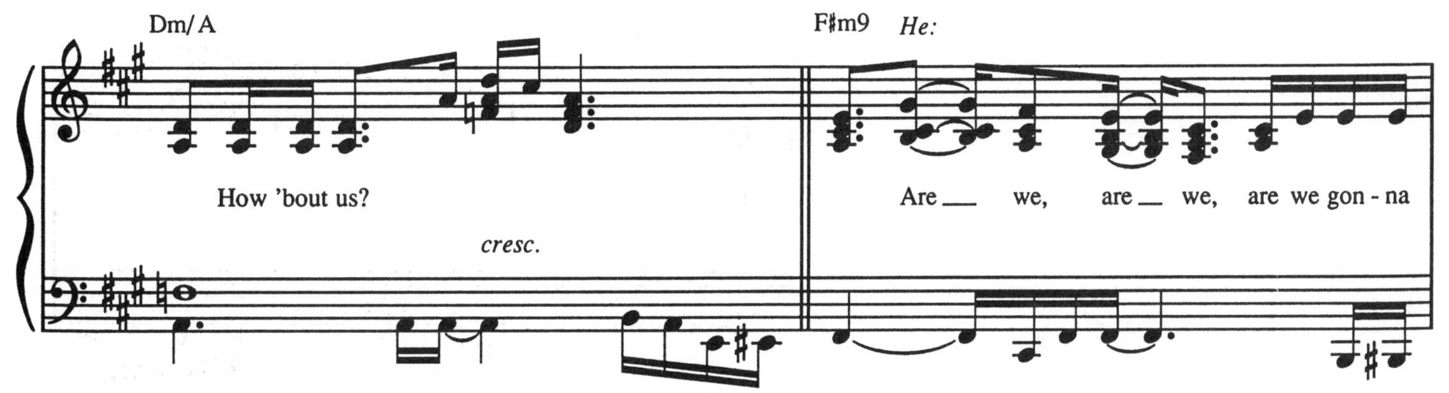
Dm/A
F♯m9
He:
How 'bout us?
cresc.
Are __ we, are __ we, are we gon - na

C♯m11
She:
He:
Both:
Em9
make it girl? _ I hope _ we can. Are we gon - na
drift, and drift, _ and drift, _ and drift, _ and

G9
C
drift to-geth - er? ______
Some peo-ple are made ___ for each oth - er;

F/C
Fm/C
some peo-ple can love _ one an-oth - er for life; ______ how 'bout

C
us?
Some peo-ple can hold it to-geth - er;

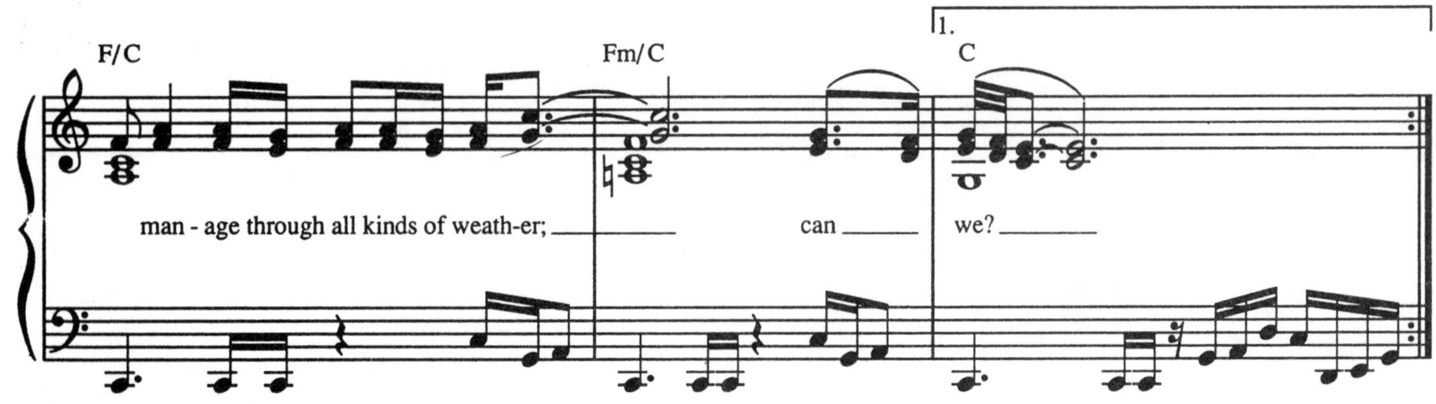
F/C
Fm/C
1.
C
man - age through all kinds of weath-er;
can
we?

2.
C
Fm/C
we?
How 'bout

C
Fm/C
Repeat ad lib. and fade
us?
How 'bout

I BELIEVE I CAN FLY

Words and Music by
R. KELLY

Dm7(♭5)/C
C
Dm7(♭5)/C
song.
But now I know the mean - ing of true love.
I'm
loud.
There are mir - a - cles in life I must a - chieve,
but
C
Dm7(♭5)/C
E7(♯5)
Bridge:
Am7
lean - ing on the ev - er - last - ing arms.
first I know it starts in - side of me.
If I can see it, then I can
Dm7(♭5)/A♭
C/G
Dm7/G
do
be
it, if I just be - lieve it, there's noth - ing to it.
I be - lieve I can
Chorus:
C
Am7
Dm7
fly, I be - lieve I can touch the sky. I think a - bout it ev - ery night and day, spread my wings and

Dm7/G
G♯dim7
Am7
Dm7(♭5)/A♭
fly a - way. I be- lieve I can soar, I see me run- ning through that o- pen door. I be- lieve I can
C/G
1.
Dm7(♭5)/A♭
Am7
fly, I be- lieve I can fly, I be- lieve I can fly.
Fmaj7/G
2.
Dm7(♭5)/A♭
Am7
2. See, fly, oh, I be- lieve I can fly.
Dm7
C/E
Fmaj7/G
Hey, 'cause I be- lieve in me, oh. If I can

Bridge:
B♭m7
E♭m7(♭5)/A
D♭/A♭
see it, then I can do it, if I just be - lieve it, there's noth - ing
Chorus:
E♭m7/A♭
D♭
B♭m7
to it. I be-lieve I can fly, I be-lieve I can touch the sky. I think a-bout it ev-ery
E♭m7
E♭m7/A♭
A dim7
night and day, spread my wings and fly a - way. I be-lieve I can
B♭m7
E♭m7(♭5)/A
soar, I see me run - ning through that o - pen door. I be-lieve I can

D♭/A♭
E♭m7(♭5)/A
D♭/A♭
fly, I be-lieve I can fly, I be-lieve I can fly, hey, if I just
E♭m7(♭5)/A
D♭/A♭
E♭m7(♭5)/A
spread my wings. I can fly, I can fly, I can
D♭/A♭
E♭m7(♭5)/A
D♭/A♭
fly, hey, if I just spread my wings. I can fly.
E♭m7(♭5)/A
D♭/A♭
E♭m7(♭5)/A
D♭
rit.

From the Touchstone Motion Picture "CON AIR"

HOW DO I LIVE

Words and Music by
DIANE WARREN

F♯m7
G♯m7
C♯m7
Em7/A
ba - by, you would take a - way ev - 'ry - thing good in my life. And tell me
Chorus:
D
A
G
F♯m7
now, how do I live with - out you? I want to know. How do I breathe with - out
Bm7
Em7
G(9)
you, if you ev - er go? How do I ev - er, ev - er sur - vive?
To Coda
1.
F♯m7/B
How do I, how do I, oh, how do I live? 2. With - out you,
2.
F♯m
how do I, oh, how do I live?

Bm7
F♯m7
F♯m7/B
If
G♯m7
C♯m7
F♯m7
you ev - er leave,
ba - by, you would take a - way ev - 'ry - thing.
G♯m7
C♯m7
F♯m7
Need you with me.
Ba - by, 'coz you know that you're ev - 'ry - thing
G♯m7
C♯m7
Em7/A
D.S. al Coda
good in my life.
And tell me

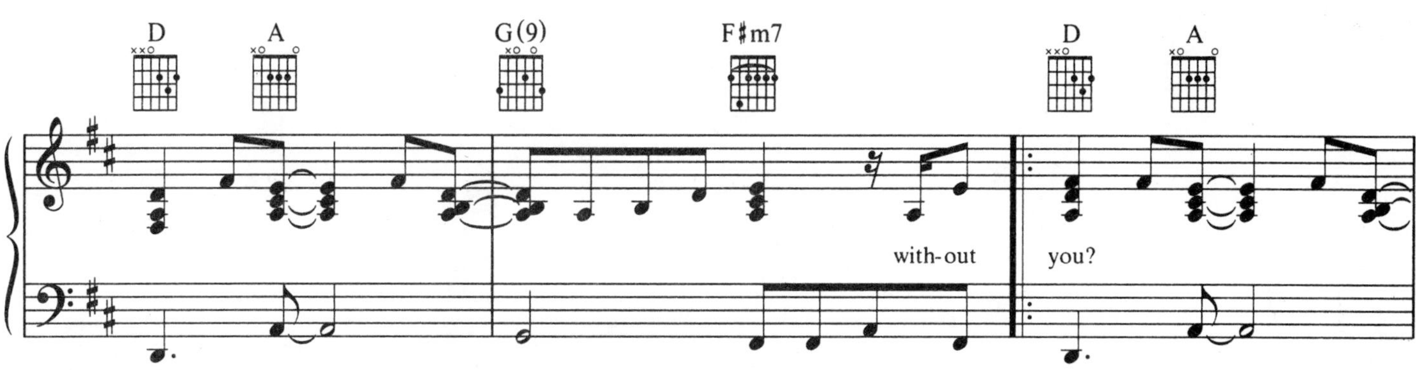

Repeat ad lib. and fade
(vocal 1st time only)

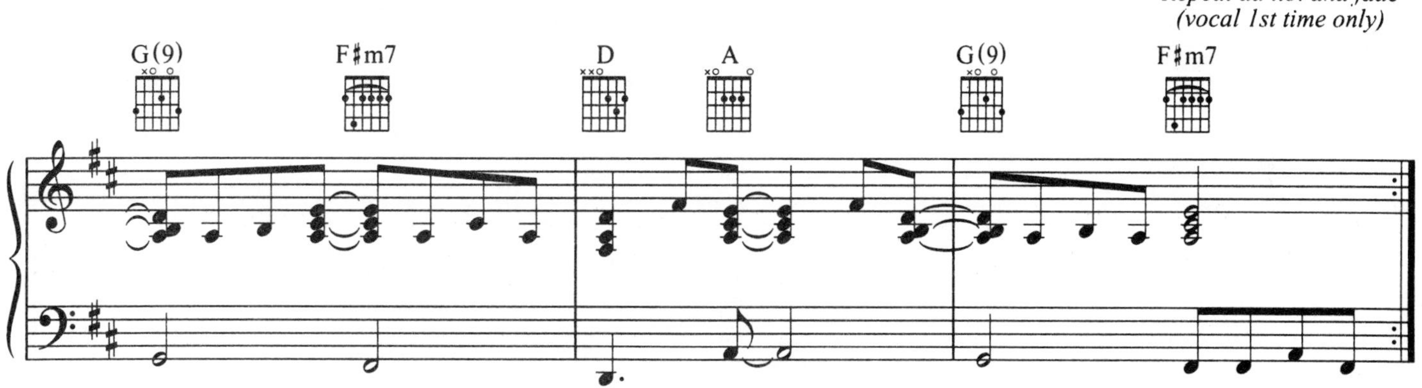

Verse 2:
Without you, there'd be no sun in my sky,
There would be no love in my life,
There'd be no world left for me.
And I, baby, I don't know what I would do,
I'd be lost if I lost you.
If you ever leave,
Baby, you would take away everything real in my life.
And tell me now...
(To Chorus:)

From the Motion Picture "THE PREACHER'S WIFE"

I BELIEVE IN YOU AND ME

Words and Music by
SANDY LINZER and DAVID WOLFERT

B
Bmaj7
D♯m7/G♯
G♯m7
D♯m7
you will al - ways be the one for me. Oh, yes, you will.
C♯m7
C♯m7/F♯
B
B/A
And I be - lieve in dreams a - gain. I be - lieve that love will nev - er end. And
E(9)/G♯
Em7
A9
B/F♯
like the riv - er finds the sea, I was lost, now I'm
D♯m7
G♯m7
C♯m7
C♯m7/F♯
1.
B
C♯m7/F♯
N.C.
free, 'cause I be - lieve in you and me. 2. I will nev - er leave

2.
Bridge:
B
D♯m7
G♯m7
D♯m7
G♯m7
me.
May-be I'm a fool to feel the way I do.
mf
C♯m7
C♯m(maj7)
C♯m7
C♯m7/F♯
N.C.
Dm7/G
I would play the fool for-ev-er just to be with you for-ev-er.
3. I be-lieve in
Verse:
C
C/B♭
Fmaj9
mir-a-cles, and love's a mir-a-cle.
And yes, ba-by, you're my dream come true.
Fm7/B♭
A♭/B♭
B♭/A♭
Fmaj7
C/G
Em7
Am7
I was lost, now I'm free, oh ba-by, 'cause

Freely

Dm7 C/E Dm7/G N.C. B♭maj7/C C Fmaj9

I be-lieve, I do___ be-lieve in you and me. See I'm lost,___ now I'm

Em7 Am7 Dm7 Dm7/G N.C.

free,___ 'cause I be - lieve_ in you_ and___ me,

a tempo

C C/B♭ Fmaj9 Dm7 Dm7/G C

be - lieve_ in you___ and me.___

rit.

Verse 2:
I will never leave your side,
I will never hurt your pride.
When all the chips are down,
I will always be around,
Just to be right where you are, my love.
Oh, I love you, boy.
I will never leave you out,
I will always let you in
To places no one has ever been.
Deep inside, can't you see?
I believe in you and me.
(To Bridge:)

I CAN LOVE YOU LIKE THAT

Words and Music by
STEVE DIAMOND, MARIBETH DERRY
and JENNIFER KIMBALL

Verse:
E♭
E♭/G
A♭(9)
read you Cin-der - el - la, you hoped it would come true; that one day your Prince Charm-ing would come
nev - er make a prom-ise I don't in-tend to keep, so when I say for - ev - er, for -
Fm7/B♭
E♭
E♭/G
res - cue you. You like ro - man - tic mov - ies, and you nev - er will for - get the
ev - er's what I mean. I'm no Ca - sa - no - va, but I swear this much is true:
A♭(9)
Fm7/B♭
Gm7
way you felt when Ro - me - o kissed Ju - li - et. And all this time that you've been wait-
I'll be hold-ing noth-ing back when it comes to you. You dream of love that's ev - er - last-
A♭(9)
Gm7
A♭(9)
- ing. You don't have to wait no more. I can love you like that,
- ing, ba - by, op - en up your eyes.

Chorus:
Eb
Eb/G
Ab(9)
I would make you my world, move heav-en and earth if you were my girl.
Fm7/Bb
Eb
Eb/G
I will give you my heart, be all that you need, show you you're ev-
Ab(9)
Eb/G
Fm7
Eb
Dbmaj9
Cm7
Fm7/Bb
-ery-thing that's pre-cious to me. If you give me a chance,
1.
Eb
Cm7
I can love you like that. I can love you like that.
I'll love you like that.

Dbmaj9
Fm7/Bb
2. Eb
2. I
I'll love you like that.
Bridge:
Bbm7
Fm7
If you want tenderness, I've got tenderness, and I
Ebsus
Eb
Ebsus
Eb
Bbm7
see through to the heart of you. If you want a man who will un-
Fm7
Ab(9)
Fm7/Bb
derstand, you don't have to look very far.

I can love you, I can love you, love you, I can love you like that,
Chorus:
E
E/G♯
A(9)
I would make you my world, move heav-en and earth if you were my girl.
F♯m7/B
E
I will give you my heart, be all that you need,
E/G♯
A(9)
Repeat ad lib. and fade
F♯m7
show you you're ev - ery-thing that's pre-cious to me. If you give me a chance,

From Touchstone Pictures' "ARMAGEDDON"

I DON'T WANT TO MISS A THING

Words and Music by
DIANE WARREN

G
D/F♯
Em7
smile while you are sleep - ing, while you're far a - way and dream - ing. I could
D
A/C♯
Bm7
G
D/F♯
spend my life in this sweet sur - ren- der. I could stay lost in this mo- ment for-
Em7
F♯m7
Gmaj7
Asus
ev - er. Ev-'ry mo- ment spent with you is a mo- ment I treas - ure.
Chorus:
D
A/C♯
Em7
Don't wan- na close my eyes, don't wan- na fall a - sleep, 'coz I'd

G
A
D
A/C♯
miss you, ba - by, and I don't wan - na miss a thing.
'Coz e - ven when I dream of you,
Em7
G
A
To Coda
the sweet - est dream would nev - er do.
I'd still miss you, ba - by, and I don't wan - na miss a thing.
D
A/C♯
Bm7
2. Lay - ing
Verse 2:
D
A/C♯
Bm7
close to you, feel - ing your heart beat - ing, and I'm
3
3

G
D/F♯
Em7
won - d'ring what you're dream - ing, won - d'ring if it's me you're see - ing. Then I
D
A/C♯
Bm7
kiss your eyes_ and thank God we're to - geth - er.___ I just wan - na
F♯m7
Gmaj7
Asus
D.S. al Coda
stay with you___ in this mo - ment for - ev - er, for - ev - er and ev - er.___
Coda
D
Bridge:
C
___ I don't wan - na miss one smile;___ I don't wan - na

G/B
B♭
miss one kiss. I just wan-na be with you, right here with you,
F/A
C
just like this. I just wan-na hold you close, feel your heart so
G/B
Dm7
close to mine, and just stay here in this mo-ment for all the
Asus
A
rest of time. Ba - by, ba - by.

Chorus:
D
A/C♯
Em7
Don't wan-na close my eyes, don't wan-na fall a-sleep, 'coz I'd
G
A
D
A/C♯
miss you, ba-by, and I don't wan-na miss a thing. 'Coz e-ven when I dream of you,
Em7
G
A
the sweet-est dream would nev-er do. I'd still miss you, ba-by, and I don't wan-na miss a thing.
D
A/C♯
Em7
Don't wan-na close my eyes, don't wan-na fall a-sleep, 'coz I'd

G
A
Bm7
A/C♯
miss you, ba - by, and I don't wan - na miss a thing.
'Coz e - ven when I dream of you,
Em7
G
A
the sweet - est dream would nev - er do.
I'd still miss you, ba - by, and I don't wan - na miss a thing.
D
A/C♯
Em7
G
A
Repeat ad lib. and fade
D
A/C♯
Em7
G
A

From the Motion Picture "THE MIRROR HAS TWO FACES"

I FINALLY FOUND SOMEONE

Words and Music by
BARBRA STREISAND, MARVIN HAMLISCH,
R.J. LANGE and BRYAN ADAMS

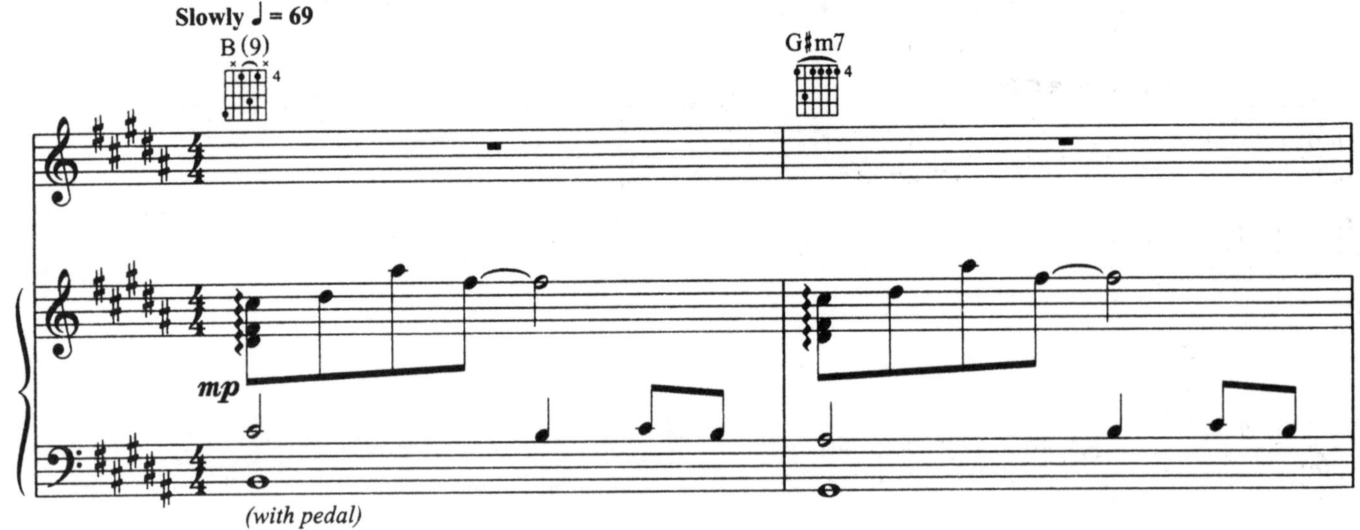

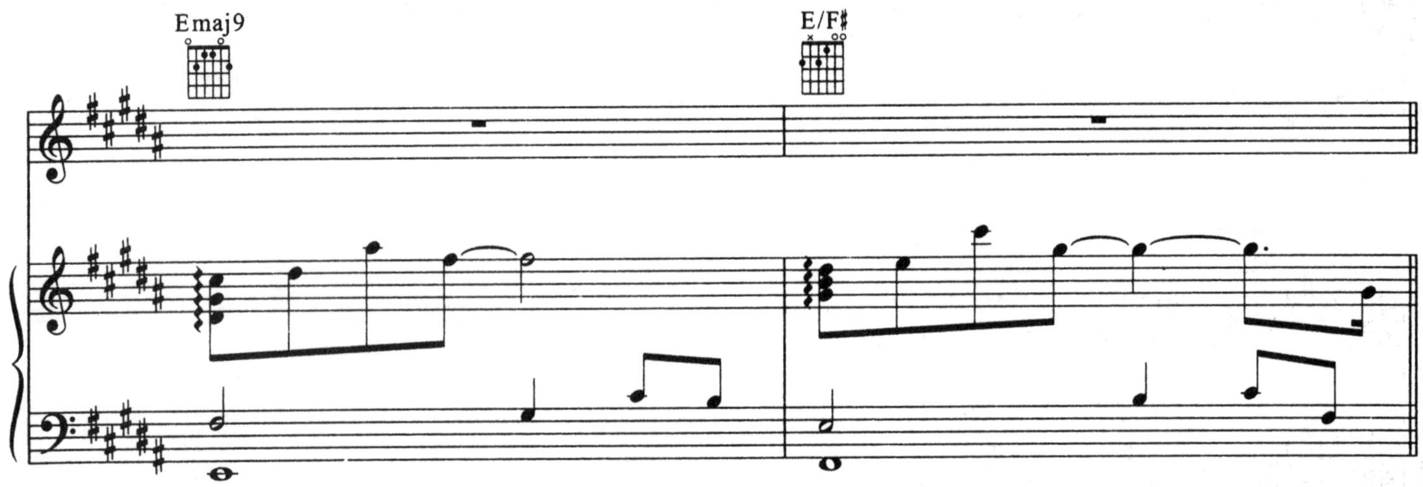

Emaj9
Em6
I fi-n'lly found the one that makes me feel com-plete.
B(9)
G♯m7
It start-ed o-ver cof-fee, we start-ed out as friends.
C♯m7/F♯
It's fun-ny how, from sim-ple things, the best things be-gin.
A♭(9)
Fm7
This time, it's dif-f'rent, it's all be-cause of you.

D♭maj9
D♭m6
It's bet-ter than it's ev - er been
'cause we can talk it
through.
through, yeah.
A♭(9)
Fm7
My fa-v'rite line was, "Can I call you some-time?"
D♭maj9
D♭m6
It's all you had to say to take my breath a - way.
Chorus:
F(9)
This is it! Oh, I fi - n'lly
mf

B♭maj9
B♭m6
F(9)
found some - one, some - one to share my life. I fi - n'lly
B♭maj9
B♭m6
F(9)
found the one to be with ev - 'ry night. 'Cause what -
A7sus
A7
Dm
D♭
ev - er I do, it's just got to be you. My
F/C
B♭/C
life has just be - gun, I fi - n'lly found some - one.

F(9) Dm7

— Ooh,— some - one,— I fi - n'lly found some - one.—

B♭maj9 F/G

— Ooh,—

Verse:

C(9) Am7

— I did - n't mind.— Ba - by, that's fine,—

Did I keep you wait - ing? I a - pol - o - gize.—

C (9)
Am7
Are you sure it looks right?
Isn't it too tight?
I love your hair,
I love what you wear.
Fmaj9
Fm6
I can't wait for the rest of my life!
Well, you're ex - cep - tion - al!
Chorus:
G♭(9)
This is it!
Oh,
I fi - n'lly
C♭maj9
C♭m6
G♭(9)
found some - one, some - one to share my life. I fi - n'lly

C♭maj9
C♭m6
G♭(9)
found the one_ to be with ev - 'ry_ night._ 'Cause what -
B♭7sus
B♭7
E♭m
ev - er I do,_ it's just got to be you.
D
G♭/D♭
Oh_ yeah, my life has just_ be - gun,_ I fi - n'lly
A♭m7/D♭
E♭7sus
E♭7
found some - one._ And what -

A♭m7
G♭/B♭
ev - er I do, it's just got to be you. Ooh, my
A♭m7/D♭
life has just be - gun, I fi - n'lly
G♭(9)
C♭maj9
found some - one.
G♭(9)

I STILL BELIEVE

Words and Music by
ANTONINA ARMATO
and BEPPE CANTORELLI

G
Am7
G/B
Cmaj7
cra - zy, but you still can touch my heart. And af - ter
D
D/C
Bm7
Em11
D
all this time, you'd think that I would - n't feel the same. But time melts in - to
Cmaj9
B7sus
B7
Em11
noth - ing, and noth - ing's changed.
Chorus:
Cmaj7
D/C
Bm7
Em11
D
I still be - lieve, some - day you and me will

Cmaj9
B7sus
B7
Am9
B7sus
B7
find our - selves in love a - gain.
Cmaj7
D/C
Bm7
Em11
D
I had a dream, some - day you and me will
Cmaj9
B7sus
B7
Am9
Am7/D
find our - selves in love a - gain. 2. Each day of my life,
Verse 2:
G
Cmaj9
D
G
Em7
D
I'm filled with all the joy I could find. You

G
Am7
G/B
Cmaj7
know that I___ am not the des - p'rate type.___ If there's one
D
D/C
Bm7
Em7
D
spark of hope___ left in my grasp,___ I'll hold it with___ both hands.___ It's worth the risk of
Cmaj9
B7sus
B7
Am7
B7sus
B7
burn - ing to have a sec - ond chance.___
Bridge:
Cmaj7
Bm7
Cmaj7
Bm7
No, no,___ no, no, no, no,___ I need you, ba - by.

Cmaj7
Bm7
A
B7sus
B7
I still be - lieve that we can be to - geth - er.
No, no, no.
If
Cmaj7
Bm7
Cmaj7
Bm7
we be - lieve that true love
nev - er has to end,
then
Cmaj7
Bm7
A
we must know that we will love a - gain.

Chorus:
Cmaj7
D/C
Bm7
Em11
D
I still be - lieve,
some - day you and me
will
Cmaj9
B7sus
B7
Am9
B7sus
B7
find our - selves in love a - gain.
Cmaj7
D/C
Bm7
Em11
D
I had a dream,
some - day you and me
will
Repeat ad lib. and fade
Cmaj9
B7sus
B7
Am9
B7sus
B7
find our - selves in love a - gain.

I WANT IT THAT WAY

Words and Music by
MAX MARTIN and
ANDREAS CARLSSON

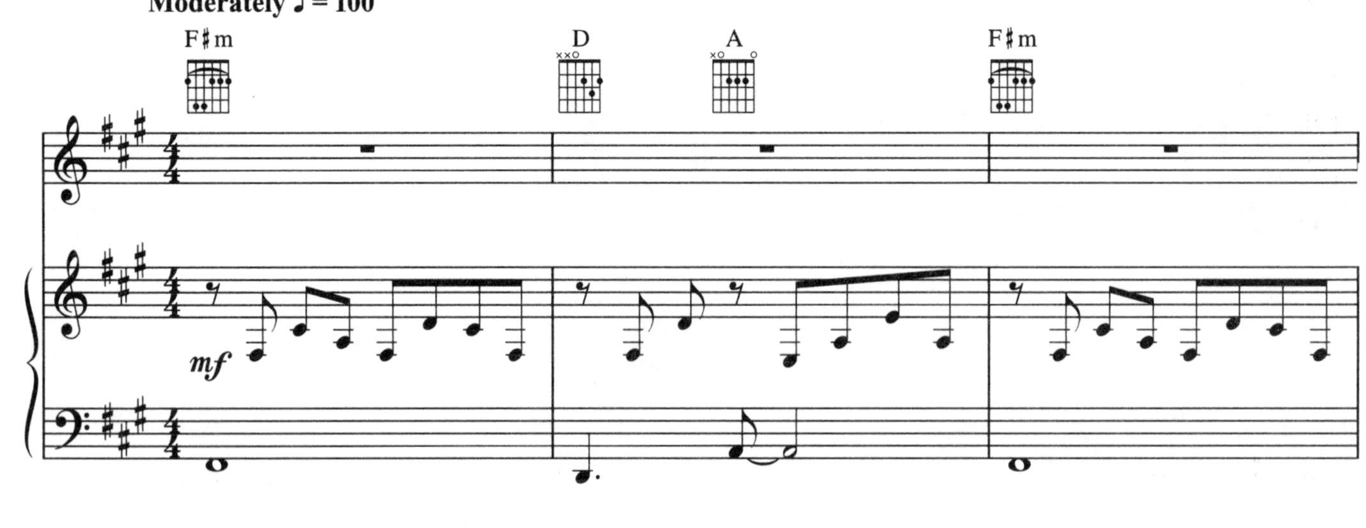

1.
D
A
F♯m
E
A
I say I want it that way. 2. But we
you say I want it
too late, but I want it
2.3.
Chorus:
E
A
D(9)
E
F♯m
that way.
that way.
Tell me why. Ain't noth-in' but a heart - ache. Tell me
D(9)
E
F♯m
D(9)
why. Ain't noth-in' but a mis - take. Tell me why. I nev-er wan-na
1.
D.S.𝄋
E
A
F♯m
E
A
hear you say I want it that way. 3. Am I

2.
Bridge:
C♯sus
C♯
F♯m
A/E
that way.
Now I can see that we've fall - en a - part from the
D
Bm
E
F♯m
way that it used to be, yeah.
No mat - ter the dis - tance, I
A/E
D
Esus
E
want you to know that deep down in - side of me you are
D(9)
E
F♯m
D(9)
my fi - re, the one de -

E
F♯m
D(9)
E
A
si - re. You are, you are, you are, you are.
F♯m
Bm
E(9)
Don't wan-na hear you say...
Ain't noth - in' but a
F♯
G♯m
E(9)
F♯
G♯m
heart - ache. Ain't noth - in' but a mis - take.
E(9)
F♯
B
G♯m
I nev - er wan-na hear you say I want it

Chorus:
F♯
B
E(9)
F♯
G♯m
that___ way.___ Tell me why.___ Ain't noth-in' but a heart - ache.___ Tell me
E(9)
F♯
G♯m
E(9)
why.___ Ain't noth-in' but a mis - take.___ Tell me why.___ I nev-er wan-na
F♯
B
G♯m
1.
F♯
B
hear you say___ I want___ it that___ way.___ Tell me
2.
F♯
B
G♯m
F♯
B
that___ way.___ 'Cause I want___ it that___ way.___
rit.

I'D LIE FOR YOU
(AND THAT'S THE TRUTH)

Words and Music by
DIANE WARREN

G(9)
A
G(9)
one who'd al - ways be a - round. Ba - by, give me a chance.
I'll take you to par - a - dise. Ain't a star that's too far.
F♯m
D
A/D
G(9)
I'd pull the sun down from the sky to light your dark - est night.
Your ev - ery wish will be a wish that I will make come true.
D
A/D
G(9)
A
I would-n't let one drop of rain fall down in - to your life. Put your heart in my hands.
And if you want the moon I'll swear I'll bring it down for you. Let me in - to your heart.
G(9)
F♯
G
Ba - by, be - lieve me I could nev - er do you wrong and I would
Be - lieve me ba - by, got your name carved on my soul, 'cause you're the

F♯
F♯7
Bm
C(9)
never paint your world blue.
only one that I'll give it to.
And if sometimes it seems I
Go let them say that I'm a
G/B
Asus
A
N.C.
must have lost my mind, I might be crazy, but I'm crazy for you.
fool to act this way, 'cause if I'm crazy, I'm just crazy 'bout you.
I'd lie for you and
I'd lie for you and
Chorus:
D
G
D/F♯
A
that's the truth.
that's the truth.
Do anything you ask me to, wo wo.
Move mountains if you want me to, wo wo.
Bm
I'd even sell my soul for you, I'd do it all for you, if
I'd walk across the fire for you, I'd walk on the wire for you, if

1.
2.
Bridge:
Em7
Asus
A
F
G
B
you'd just be - lieve in me.
you'd just be - lieve in
me. And you will ne - ver see a day I'll ev - er break your heart, you'll see the
sky fall down be - fore it ev - er gets that far. I'll show you heav - en ev - ery se - cond that you're
in my arms. Ba - by, I'm cra - zy, but I'm cra - zy 'bout you.

A/B
E
A
E/G♯
B
N.C.
I'd lie for you and
that's the truth.
that's the truth.
Do an - y - thing you
Move moun-tains if you
E
A
E/G♯
B
C♯m
B
ask me to, wo wo.
want me to, wo wo.
I'd e - ven sell my soul for you,
I'd walk a - cross the fire for you,
I'd do it all
I'd walk on the
A
E/G♯
1.
F♯m7
B
for you,
wire for you,
if you'd just be - lieve in me.
if
I'd lie for you and
2.
F♯m7
Bsus
B
E
freely
you'd just be - lieve in me.
I'd lie for you and that's the truth.

I'LL BE THERE FOR YOU
(Theme from "FRIENDS")

Words by
DAVID CRANE, MARTA KAUFFMAN, ALLEE WILLIS,
PHIL SOLEM and DANNY WILDE

Music by
MICHAEL SKLOFF

C♯m
G
love life's D. O. A.
things are go - ing great.
(1.3.) It's like you're al -
(2.) Your moth - er warned
Bm
A
ways stuck in sec - ond gear.
you there'd be days like these.
Well, it
But she
G
D/F♯
Esus
has n't been your day, your week, your month, or e - ven your
did n't tell you when the world has brought you down to your
1.2.
To Next Strain
E
3.
year. But
knees, that
year.
Chorus:
A
D
E
I'll be there for you when the

* Guitar fill reads 8va.

er know — me,
no one could ev - er see — me.

F♯m
Seems you're the on - ly one — who knows — what it's

Bm
like to be — me. Some - one to face — the day — with,

D/A
G
make it through all — the rest — with, some - one I'll al -

G/F♯
E
D
E
ways laugh with.
E - ven at my worst,
I'm best with
F♯m
(1st time only)
D
E
you.
Yeah!
(Inst. solo ad lib....
A
D
To Coda
1.
2.
D.S. al Coda
E
D/F♯
...end solo)

Coda

Chorus:

A D

I'll___ be there for___ you___

E A

___ I'll___ be

D E

there for___ you___

A D E

___ I'll___ be there for___ you___ 'cause you're

D/F♯ G A

there for___ me, too.___

I'LL NEVER BREAK YOUR HEART

By
ALBERT MANNO and
EUGENE WILDE

B♭
Gm7
asked you out, you said no, but I found out, darling,
E♭
F
E♭
D7/F♯
that you'd been hurt, you felt that you'd nev - er love a - gain.
Gm
Gm(maj7)
Gm7
Gm6
I de-serve a try, hon - ey, just once, give me a chance and I'll prove this all wrong. You walked
Dm7
G7(♯5)
1.
To Next Strain
Cm7
Dm7
Cm7/E♭
Cm7/F
in, you were so quick to judge, but hon - ey, he's noth-ing like me. I'll nev - er

2.
Cm7
Dm7
Cm7/E♭
E♭/F
hon - ey, he's noth - ing like me. Dar - ling, why can't you see? I'll nev - er
Chorus:
B♭
Gm
break your heart, I'll nev - er make you cry. I'd rath - er
E♭
Dm7
G7(♯5)
Cm7
Cm7/F
die than live with - out you, I'll give you all of me, hon - ey, that's no lie. I'll nev - er
B♭
Gm
break your heart, I'll nev - er make you cry. I'd rath - er

Eb
Dm7
G7(#5)
Cm7
Cm7/F
die than live with - out you, I'll give you all of me, hon - ey, that's no lie.
Bridge:
Dm7
D7
Gm
F
Gm
No way, no how, I swear,
(I'll never make you cry.)
Dm7
D7
Eb
Eb/F
E/F#
no way, no how. I, I'll nev - er
Chorus:
B
G#m
break your heart, I'll nev - er make you cry. I'd rath - er

Verse 2:
As I walked by you,
Will you get to know me
A little more better?
Girl, that's the way love goes.
And I know you're afraid
To let your feelings show,
And I understand.
But girl, it's time to let go.

I deserve a try, honey,
Just once,
Give me a chance
And I'll prove this all wrong.
You walked in,
You were so quick to judge,
But honey, he's nothing like me.
Darling, why can't you see?
(To Chorus:)

IT'S NOT RIGHT BUT IT'S OKAY

Words and Music by
RODNEY JERKINS, FRED JERKINS III,
LaSHAWN DANIELS, ISAAC PHILLIPS
and TYE-V TURMAN

Cm
eat.
week, yes, I am.
that, tell me?
Fm
Then they hung out,
The phone rings
See, I'm mov - in' on
Cm
but you came home a - round three, yes, you did.
and then you look at me.
and I re - fuse to turn back, yeah.
Fm
If six of y'all went out,
You said it was one of your friends
See, all of this time,

Cm
then four of you were real - ly cheap,
down on Fif - ty - Fourth Street,
I thought I had some - bod - y down for a man.
Fm
To Coda I
yeah. 'Cause on - ly two of you had din - ner. I
yeah. So why did 2 1 3
It turns out, you
Cm
To Coda II
Chorus:
Fm7
found your cred - it card re - ceipt.
were mak - ing a fool of me.
It's not right, but it's o -
Cm
kay. I'm gon - na make it an - y - way. Pack your

Fm7
Cm
bags, up and leave. Don't you dare come run - ning back to
Fm7
me. It's not right, but it's o - kay. I'm gon - na
Cm
Fm7
make it an - y - way. Close the door be - hind you, leave your
Cm
D.S. 𝄋 al Coda I
key. I'd rath - er be a - lone than un - hap - py.

Coda I
Cm
Bridge:
Fm7
show up on your call-er I. D.? I've been through all of this be-fore,
Cm7
no mat-ter what you think.
I won't stand a-
Fm7
Cm7
round and take some more,
things are gon-na change.
B♭m7
E♭7
Fm7
You don't e-ven stand a chance no more
'cause now you've got to

Cm7
Fm7
leave. So don't turn a - round to see my face.
Cm7
D.S.𝄋 al Coda II
There's no more tears left here for you to
Chorus:
ΦΦCoda II
Fm7
right, but it's o - kay. I'm gon - na
Cm
Fm7
make it an - y - way. Pack your bags, up and

Cm
leave. Don't you dare come run - ning back to me. It's not
Fm7
Cm
right, but it's o - kay. I'm gon - na make it an - y -
Fm7
way. Close the door be - hind you, leave your key. I'd rath - er be a -
Cm
Repeat ad lib. and fade
lone than un - hap - py. It's not

KAREN'S THEME

Composed by
RICHARD CARPENTER

F
B♭/F
To Coda
F
Dm7
a tempo
G
C/G
G7sus(♭9)
G7
rit.
C/G
C
B♭/C
C9
a tempo
B♭
C
B♭/C
C
F/C
F
Am
F♯m7(♭5)
B7

D.S. 𝄋 al Coda
Em7
A7sus
A7
Gm7(♭5)
C7sus(♭9)
Csus
rit.
pp
Coda
F
F/A
B♭
D7(♭9)
Gm
Gm7(♭5)
rit.
F/C
G/C
C7sus
freely
C
F
B♭
F
G9
F
a tempo
rit.
Ped.
Ped.
Ped.
Ped.

LIVE AND LET DIE

Words and Music by
PAUL McCARTNEY and
LINDA McCARTNEY

D
Bb
G7
C
(G bass)
give it a cry,
Say live and let die!
Live and let
Gdim
G7
C
(G bass)
die,
Live and let
die,
Live and let
die.
Gm
3fr
ff
C9
To Coda
8va lower ad lib. till *
What does it mat - ter to ya,
mf

G7
D7
when you got a job to do you got-ta do it well, You got-ta
Em
F
Gm
3fr
give the oth-er fel-low hell!
ff
D. C. al Coda
Coda
Gm
3fr
Eb m
(Gb bass)
T

KISSING YOU
(Love Theme From "ROMEO + JULIET")

Words and Music by
DES'REE and TIM ATACK

Dm7
C(9)
Am7
Em7
Am7
C/G
Dm7
Am7
G/B
Heav - ing heart is full of pain,
oh, oh, the
Chorus:
C
G/B
G♯dim7
Am7
Dm7
Am7
G/B
ach - ing.
'Cause I'm kiss - ing
C
G/B
Am7
C/G
Dm7
Am7
G/B
C
G/B
Am7
C/G
you, oh. I'm kiss-ing you.
Verse:
Dm7
C(9)
Am7
Em7
Am7
C/G
Dm7
Am7
G/B
2. Touch me deep, pure, and true, gift to me for-

Chorus:
C
G/B
Am7
C/G
Dm7
Am7
G/B
C
G/B
Am7
C/G
ev - er.
'Cause I'm
kiss - ing
you,
oh.
Dm7
Am7
G/B
C
G/B
Am7
C/G
Dm7
C
I'm
kiss - ing
you.
Am7
C/G
Dm7
C
Am7
C/G
Fmaj7
G
Am7
G/B

Dm9
C
G/B
Am7
Dm7
Am7
freely
Where are you now?
rit.
C
G/B
Am7
C/G
Dm7
Am7
Where are you now?
'Cause
I'm kiss-ing you.
I'm kiss - ing
C(9)
Am9
you, oh.

LET'S MAKE A NIGHT TO REMEMBER

Words and Music by
BRYAN ADAMS and ROBERT JOHN "MUTT" LANGE

G Am7 F(9)

-ery-thing but talk__ and how ya stare at me with those un-dress me eyes.__

C Gsus G *Bridge:* Am

Your breath__on my bod-y makes me warm in-side.__ Let's make out,

F G C

let's do some-thing a-maz-ing, let's do some-thing that's all__

Em7 G F(9)

__ the way,____ cuz I nev-er touched some-bod-y like the

G
N.C.
way I touch your bod - y, now I nev - er want to let your bod - y go. Let's make a
Chorus:
C
F(9)
C
night to re - mem - ber, from Jan - u - ar - y to De -
F(9)
C
F(9)
cem - ber. Let's make love to ex - cite us, a mem - o -
C
F(9)
G
ry to ig - nite us. Let's make hon - ey, ba - by, soft and

F
G
F
ten - der. Let's make sug - ar, dar - lin', sweet sur - ren - der. Let's make a
C
F(9)
To Coda
C
night to re - mem - ber all life long.
Csus
C
G
Verse:
C
Csus
C
2. I love the way ya move to - night, beads of sweat drip - pin' down.

G7sus
G
Em7
F(9)
— your skin._
Me ly - in' here,
'n' you ly - in' there,_
G7sus
G
D.S. % al Coda
Coda
N.C.
our sha - dows on the wall and our
hands_
ev - ery - where._ Let's make
long._
F(9)
G
Am
C
F(9)
G
C
Oh,_
well, I
think a - bout ya all of the time._
Can't you

G
Am7
F
see you drive me out-ta my mind?
Well, I'm nev-er hold-in' back a-gain.
Dm
F
G
Yeah, I nev-er want this night to end,
cuz I've
F(9)
G
N.C.
nev-er touched some-bod-y like the way I touch your bod-y, now I nev-er want to let your bod-y go.
D
G(9)
D
Let's make a night to re-mem-ber, from Jan-u-ar-y to De-

G(9)
D
G(9)
cem - ber. Let's make love to ex - cite us, a mem - o -
D
G(9)
A
ry to ig - nite us. Let's make hon - ey, ba - by, soft and
G
A
G
ten - der. Let's make sug - ar, dar - lin', sweet sur - ren - der. Let's make a
D
G(9)
N.C.
night to re - mem - ber all, all life long.

D
Dsus
D
A
D/F♯
G
Oh, let's make out,
let's do some-thing a - maz -
D/A
A
Bm7
- ing,
let's do some-thing that's all
the way,
G(9)
D
A
Repeat ad lib. and fade
ev - ery day.

LIVIN' LA VIDA LOCA

Words and Music by
ROBI ROSA and DESMOND CHILD

Verse 1:

1. She's in - to su - per - sti - tions, black cats and voo-doo dolls.

I feel a pre-mo-ni-tion, that girl's gon-na make me fall.
Verses 2 & 3:
2. She's in-to new sen-sa-tions, new kicks in the can-dle-light.
3. See additional lyrics
She's got a new ad-dic-tion for ev-'ry day and night. 1. She'll

Bridge:
F♯m
G♯m
(3.) make you take your clothes off and go danc - ing in the rain. She'll make
2. See additional lyrics
A
B
you live her cra - zy life, but she'll take a - way your pain,
G♯7sus
like a bul - let to your brain.
Chorus:
C♯m
B
Up - side, in - side out, she's liv - in' la vi - da lo -

C♯m
ca. She'll push and pull you down,
B
C♯m
liv - in' la vi - da lo - ca. Her lips are dev -
B
C♯m
il red and her skin's the col - or of mo - cha.
B
She will wear you out, liv - in' la vi - da lo -

C♯m
B
C♯m
ca,
liv - in' la vi - da lo - ca.
She's
B
To Coda
C♯m
liv - in' la vi - da lo - ca.
(Inst. solo ad lib. . . .
1.
2.
D.S. al Coda
. . . end solo)
3. She'll

Coda
C♯m
ca.
Up - side, in - side out, she's
2. Instrumental (Vocal ad lib.)
B
C♯m
liv - in' la vi - da lo - ca.
She'll push and pull
B
C♯m
you down,
liv - in' la vi - da lo - ca.
Her
B
lips are dev - il red and her skin's the col - or of mo -

Verse 3:
Woke up in New York City
In a funky, cheap hotel.
She took my heart and she took my money.
She must have slipped me a sleeping pill.

Bridge 2:
She never drinks the water
And makes you order French champagne.
Once you've had a taste of her
You'll never be the same.
Yeah, she'll make you go insane.
(To Chorus:)

MENTAL PICTURE

Words and Music by
JON SECADA and
MIGUEL A. MOREJON

G2
A
G
A
G2
can't I feel?) Say-ing my
blind side.
And if a
Chorus:
D
A/D
Dsus
D
A/B
men - tal pic - ture's all I got to go
C(9)
3
G
on, for a
while or more, girl, you
know I'll al - ways think
Asus
A
D
A/D
Dsus
of you,
think of you.
And if a
men - tal pic -
D
A/B
- ture's all I've got to go on,
I know your a

Verse 2:
Time was of the essence,
And as usual the day turns into minutes.
Sharing love and tenderness,
That's the nerve you struck in me that sent a signal.
To the other side,
(Girl, I don't know,)
Saying my blind side.
And if a . . . *(To Chorus:)*

MMMBOP

Words and Music by
ISAAC HANSON, TAYLOR HANSON
and ZAC HANSON

Verse:
A
E
D
E
1. You have so man - y re - la - tion - ships_ in this life, on - ly one or two_ will last._
You go through all the pain_ and strife,_ then you turn your back_ and they're gone so fast._
Oh yeah,
and they're gone_
so_ fast,
yeah._

Verse:

A E D E

2. So hold on to the ones who real - ly care,___ in the end___ they'll be the on - ly ones there.___
3. Plant a seed, plant a flow - er, plant___ a rose.___ You can plant an - y one of those.___

A E D E

When you get old___ and start los - ing your hair,___ can you tell me who___ will still___
Keep plant - ing to find out which one grows. It's a se - cret no___ one knows.___

A E D E

care?___ Can you tell me who___ will___
It's a se - cret no___ one___

A E D E

still care? Oh,___ oh ca - are.___
knows. Oh,___ no one knows.___

𝄋 Chorus:
A
D
A
Mmm bop, ba du-ba dop_ ba du bop, ba du-ba dop ba du bop, ba du-ba dop_ ba
E
A
D
du._ Yeah._ Mmm bop, ba du-ba dop_ ba du bop, ba du-ba dop ba
To Coda
1.
A
E
A
E
du bop, ba du-ba dop_ ba du._ Yeah._ Said, oh_ yeah,_
D
E
A
E
D
E
in an mmm_ bop, they're gone. Yeah,_ yeah._ Yeah._

2.
A
E
D
E
In an mmm_ bop, they're gone,__
in an mmm_ bop, they're not there._
__ In an mmm_ bop, they're gone,
in an mmm_ bop, they're not there.
__ Un-til you lose_ your hair,__
ooh,__
but they don't care
'n' yeah, yeah.__
D.S. 𝄋 al Coda
Coda
du.__
Yeah.__
Can you tell_ me?
No, you can't_ 'cause you don't know._

A E D E A E

Can you tell me? You say you can, but you don't know. Can you tell me which

D E A E D E

flow-er's go-ing to grow? Can you tell me if it's gon-na be a dai-sy or a rose?

A E D E A E

You say you can, but you don't know. You don't know,

D E A N.C. D N.C.

you don't know, oh. Mmm bop, du bop.

A
N.C.
E
A
N.C.
Mmm bop du. Yeah. Mmm bop,
D
N.C.
A
N.C.
E
du bop. Mmm bop du. Yeah.
A
D
Mmm bop, ba du - ba dop ba du bop, ba du - ba dop ba
A
E
Repeat ad lib. and fade
du bop, ba du - ba dop ba du. Yeah.

REACH

Words and Music by
GLORIA ESTEFAN and
DIANE WARREN

Reach - 5 - 1

Cm7
Fm7
do_ what-ev - er it_ takes,_ fol - low through_
go_ the dis - tance this_ time,_ see - ing more_
Cm7
Fm7
_ with the prom - ise I_ made,_ put it
_ the high - er I_ climb_ that the
G♭
Fm7/B♭
all on the line,_ what I hope for at last_ would be mine_
more I be - lieve,_ all the more that this dream_ will be mine_
if I could
cresc.
Chorus:
E♭
B♭
reach high - er,_ just for one
mf

Fm7
A♭
B♭sus
B♭
mo - ment, touch the sky, from that one mo - ment in my life, I'm gon - na
E♭
B♭
be strong - er, know that I've
Fm7
A♭
B♭sus
B♭
tried my ver - y best, I'd put my spir - it to the test, if I could
1.
A♭
E♭
reach...
dim.

2.
C♭maj7
B♭m7
reach...
C♭maj7
B♭sus
B♭
C
If I could
Chorus:
F
C
reach
high - er,
just for one
Gm7
B♭
Csus
C
mo - ment, touch the sky,
from that one
mo - ment in my life,
I'm gon - na

F
C
be
strong - er,
know that I've
Gm7
1.
B♭
Csus
C
tried my ver - y best,
I'd put my spir - it to the test,
if I could
2.
B♭
Csus
C
F
spir - it to the test,
if I could
reach...
N.C.
dim.
mp

MORE THAN WORDS

Lyrics and Music by
BETTENCOURT, CHERONE

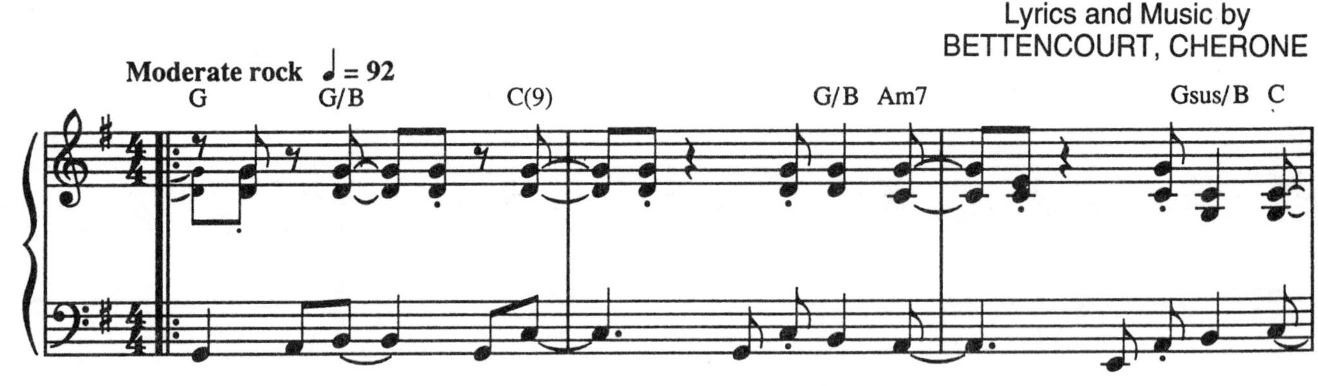

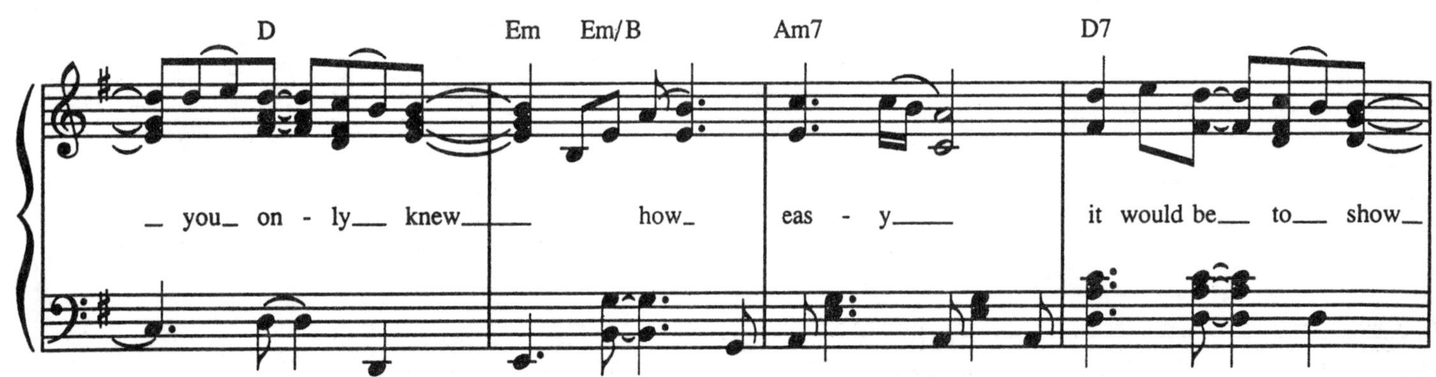

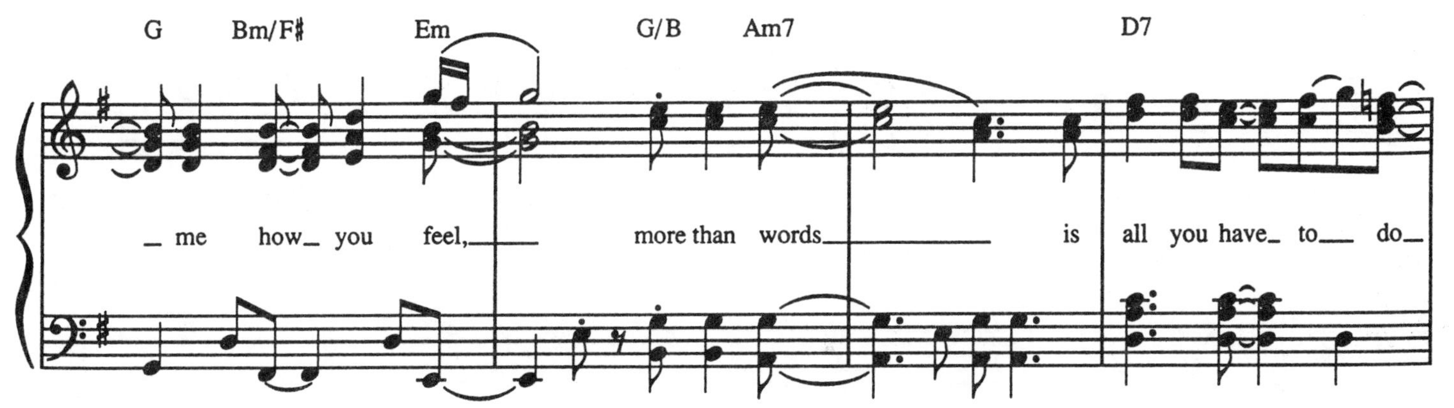
G
Bm/F♯
Em
G/B
Am7
D7
_ me how_ you feel,___ more than words_______ is all you have_ to_ do_

G7
G7/B
C
Cm
G
Em7
_ to make_ it_ real.___ Then, you would - n't have_ to say_______ that you love_

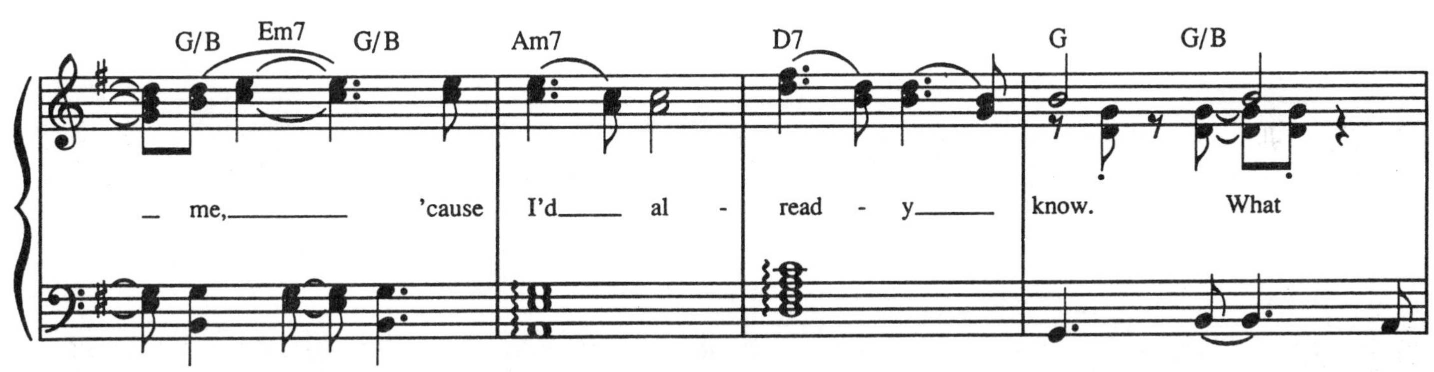
G/B
Em7
G/B
Am7
D7
G
G/B
_ me,_______ 'cause I'd___ al - read - y___ know. What

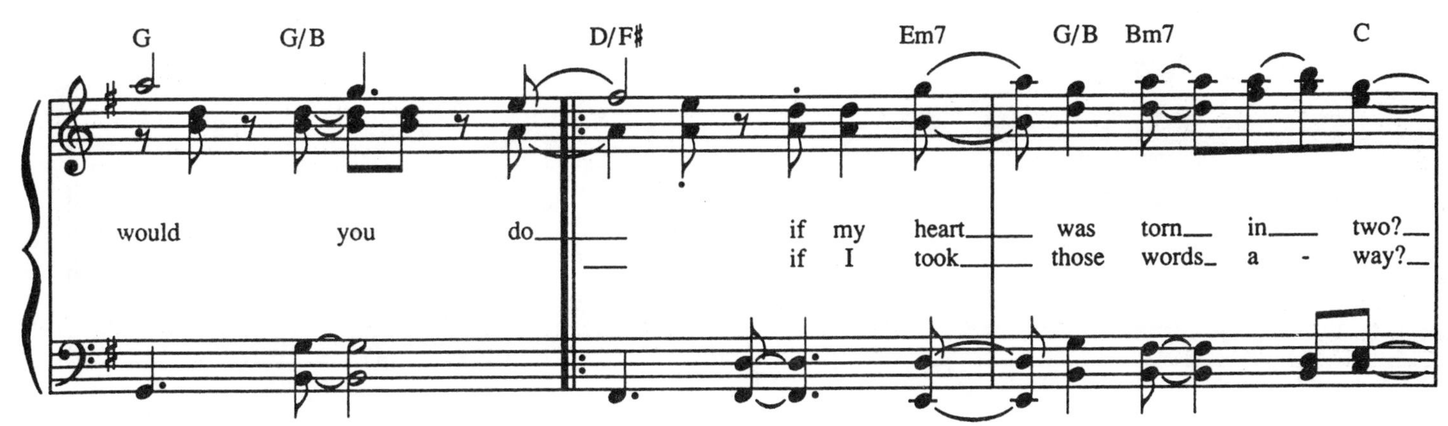
G
G/B
D/F♯
Em7
G/B
Bm7
C
would you do___ if my heart___ was torn__ in__ two?__
___ if I took___ those words_ a - way?__

1. 3.
G/B Am7
D7
G
More than words to show you feel that your love for me is real.
Then, you could - n't make things new just by say -

2.
To Next Strain
4.
G/B
G
G/B
D7
D7
What would you say
- in' "I love you."
- in' "I love you."

G
G/B
C(9)
G/B
Am7
G/B
C
(La di da da di da di dai dai da.

1.
D.S. 𝄋
D
D7
G
G/B
C(9)
Am7
D7
) More than words.
La di da da di da.)

Verse 2:
Now that I have tried to talk to you
And make you understand.
All you have to do is close your eyes
And just reach out your hands.
And touch me, hold me close, don't ever let me go.
More than words is all I ever needed you to show.
Then you wouldn't have to say
That you love me 'cause I'd already know.
(To Chorus:)

From the Miramax Motion Picture "Music Of The Heart"

MUSIC OF MY HEART

Words and Music by
DIANE WARREN

F♯7sus
F♯7
B
B/D♯
G♯m7
done for my soul.
see - ing me through.
You'll nev - er know the gift you've
You were the song that al - ways
E
B/D♯
giv - en me. I'll car - ry it with me.
made me sing. I'm sing - ing this for you.
C♯m7
B/D♯
Through the days a - head, I think of days be - fore, when you made me
Ev - 'ry - where I go, I think of where I've been and of the

Amaj9
C♯m7/F♯
hope for some - thing bet - ter and made me reach for some - thing more.
one who knew me bet - ter than an - y - one ev - er will a - gain.
You taught me to run,
Chorus:
B
F♯/A♯
C♯m7
you taught me to fly, helped me to free the me in - side. Helped me hear the
E
B/D♯
C♯m7
C♯m7/F♯
mu - sic of my heart. Helped me hear the mu - sic of my heart. You o-pened my
B
F♯/A♯
Amaj9
eyes, you o-pened the door to some-thing I've nev - er known be-fore. And your

1.
C♯m7
C♯m7/F♯
A2
love is the mu - sic of my heart.
2.
Bridge:
C♯m7
C♯m7/F♯
E
F♯
love is the mu - sic of my heart. What you taught me, on - ly
E/G♯
F♯/A♯
B
your love could ev - er teach me. You got through where no one could reach me be - fore.
(Be -
E
C♯m7
Coz you al - ways saw in me all the best
fore.)

B/D♯
Amaj9
C♯m7/F♯
— that I — could be. —
It was you — who set — me free. — You taught me to run, —
B
F♯/A♯
C♯m7
— you taught me to fly, — helped me to free — the me — in - side. — Helped me hear the
E
B/D♯
C♯m7
B/D♯
C♯m7/F♯
E♭m7/A♭
mu - sic of — my heart. Helped me hear the mu - sic of — my heart. You taught me to run, —
Chorus:
D♭
A♭/C
E♭m7
— you taught me to fly, — helped me to free — the me — in - side. — Helped me hear the

G♭
D♭/F
E♭m7
D♭
A♭/C
E♭m7/A♭
music of my heart. Helped me hear the music of my heart. You opened my
D♭
A♭/C
C♭maj9
eyes, you opened the door to something I've never known before. And your
E♭m7
E♭m7/A♭
C♭2
love is the music of my heart,
rit.
D♭
is the music of my heart.

ONCE IN A LIFETIME

Words and Music by
WALTER AFANASIEFF, MICHAEL BOLTON
and DIANE WARREN

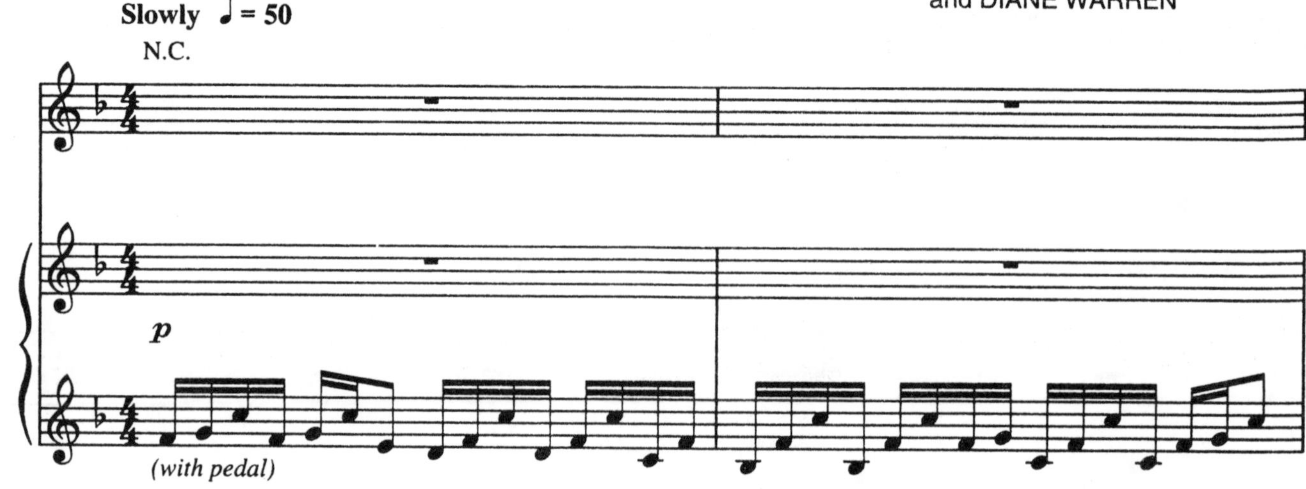

Slowly ♩ = 50

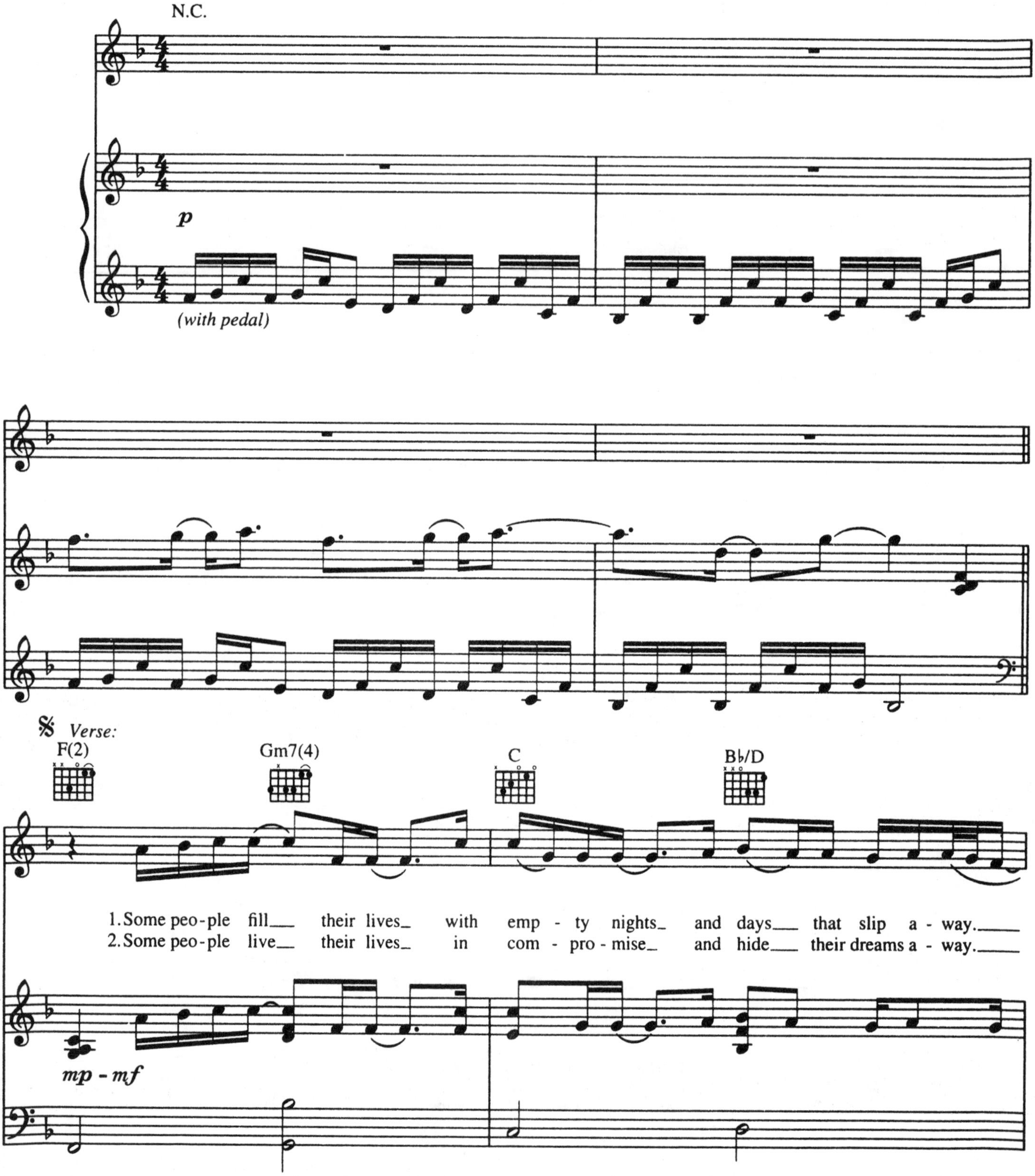
N.C.
p
(with pedal)
Verse:
F(2)
Gm7(4)
C
B♭/D
1. Some peo - ple fill their lives with emp - ty nights and days that slip a - way.
2. Some peo - ple live their lives in com - pro - mise and hide their dreams a - way.
mp - mf

Dm Gm7 C A7/C♯

Some search till the end of time, but nev - er find the o - pen arms of fate.
Some nev - er take the chance with - in their hands to claim the prize they make.

Dm Fmaj7/C Bm7(♭5) N.C.

One mo - ment comes a - long, and some - one hands your
When faith is all you need to hold the hand of

B♭6 B♭m(maj7) Gm7/C C7

dreams to you, and all at once your dreams come true.
des - ti - ny, and find the love that's meant to be.
Once in a life -

Chorus:

F C/E Dm B♭/D C7/E F

- time, you find the one you real - ly love, for

Dm
F/A
Gm7
C7sus
now and for - ev - er, one love that nev - er ends. Once in a life-
F
C/E
Dm
B♭/D
C7/E
A7/C♯
Dm
- time, when ev-'ry star that lights the sky will
F/A
B♭(2)
Gm7(4)
Gm7
B♭/C
shine with one rea - son, lead-ing your heart to the one love you find just once in a
1.
F
C/E
Dm7
B♭(2)
C7sus
D.S. 𝄋
life - time.

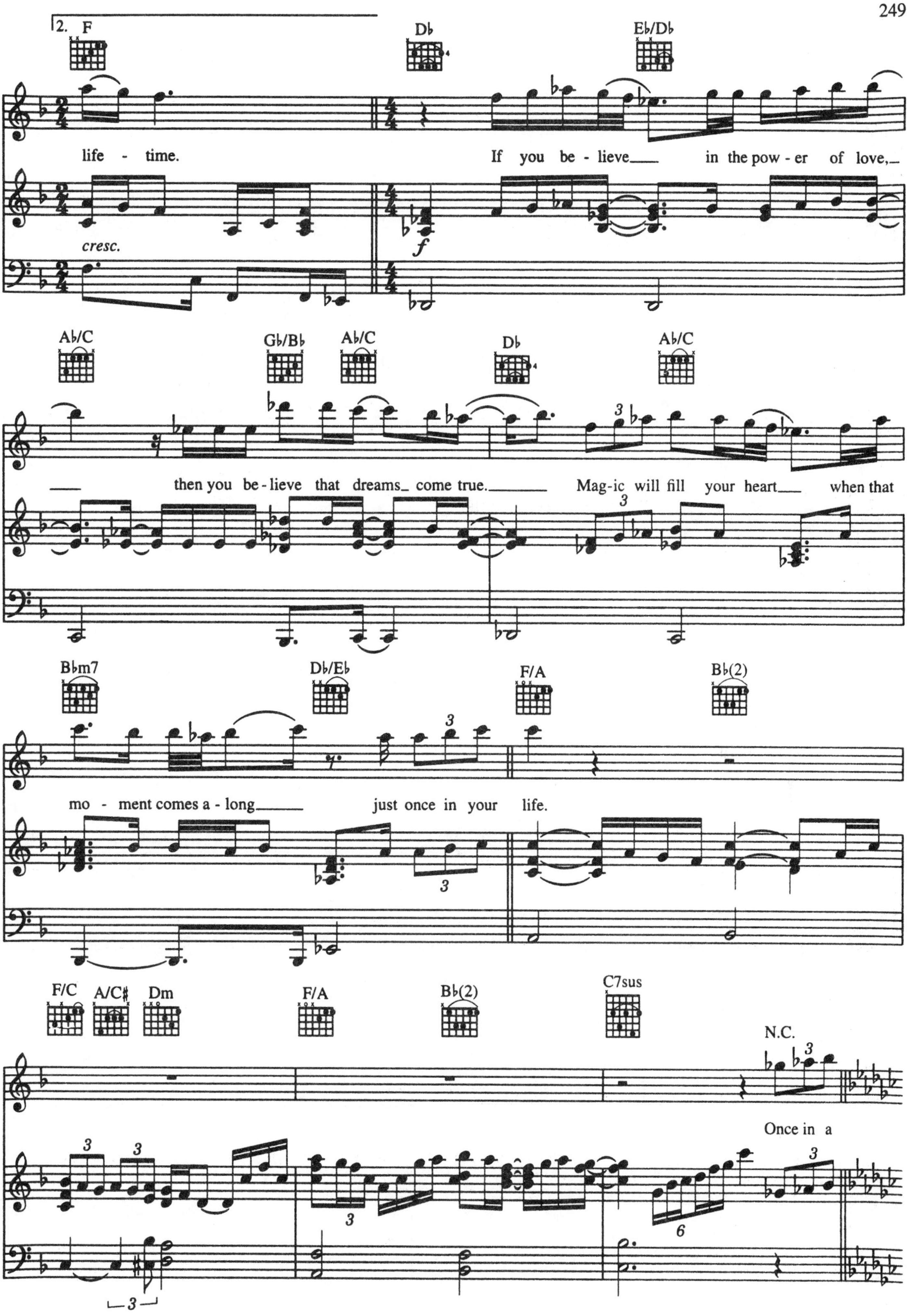

2. F — D♭ — E♭/D♭

life - time. If you be - lieve in the pow - er of love,

cresc.

f

A♭/C — G♭/B♭ — A♭/C — D♭ — A♭/C

then you be - lieve that dreams come true. Mag - ic will fill your heart when that

B♭m7 — D♭/E♭ — F/A — B♭(2)

mo - ment comes a - long just once in your life.

F/C — A/C♯ — Dm — F/A — B♭(2) — C7sus — N.C.

Once in a

Gb
Db/F
Ebm
Cb/Db
Db/F
Gb
life-time,
you find the one you real - ly love,
for
Ebm
Gb/Bb
Abm7
Db7sus
now and for-ev - er,
one love that nev - er ends.
Once in a life-
Gb
Db/F
Ebm
Fm7(b5)
Bb7
Ebm
- time,
when ev-'ry star that lights the sky
will
Cb
Gb/Bb
Abm7(4)
Abm7
Cb/Db
shine with one rea - son,
lead-ing you home to the
one love you'll find
just once in a

Gb Db/F Ebm7 Cb(2) Dbsus

mp

life - time. Just once in a life -

Gb Db/F Ebm7 Cb(2) Dbsus

- time.____ Once in a life -

Gb(2) Ebm7 Gb/Bb Cb(2) Dbsus

- time._ (2nd time, begin ad lib. vocals) Once in a life -

Gb(2) Ebm7 Gb/Bb Cb(2)

Repeat ad lib. and fade

- time._ Once in a life -

THE PRAYER

Italian Lyric by
ALBERTO TESTA and TONY RENIS

Words and Music by
CAROLE BAYER SAGER and DAVID FOSTER

F/A
B♭
Gm/C
and help us to be wise
in times when we don't
E♭/F
F
poco rit.
know.
Let this be our
poco rit.
Chorus:
Gm
Gm7/C
C7
A7sus
a tempo
prayer,
when we lose our way.
a tempo
A7
Dm
B♭
Dm
Am
Lead us to a place,
guide us with your grace

B♭ F/C C B♭/F F
to a place where we'll be safe.
Male:
mf
La lu - ce che tu
mf
Verse 2:
B♭ C7sus C7 F
mf
I pray we'll find your light, and hold it in our
dai, nel cuo - re res - te - rá.
F/A B♭ Csus C Gm/C C
hearts when stars go out each night,
A ri - cor - dar - ci che l'e - ter - na ste - lla

E♭/F
F7
poco rit.
oh.
cresc.
poco rit.
sei.
Ne - lla mia pre -
cresc.
poco rit.
Chorus:
a tempo
Gm
Gm7/C
C7
A7sus
Let this be our prayer,
when sha - dows fill our
a tempo
ghie - ra
quan - ta fe - de c'é.
a tempo
f
A7
Dm
B♭
Dm
Am
mp
day.
guide us with your grace.
mp
Lead us to a place,
dim.
mp

B♭
F/C
C7
B♭/F
F
cresc.
Give us faith so we'll be safe.
So - gna - mo un
cresc.
Give us faith so we'll be safe.
So - gna - mo un
cresc.
Bridge:
C/B♭
B♭
C/B♭
Fsus
F
C/B♭
B♭
C/B♭
mf
mon - do sen - za piú vio - len - za. Un mon - do di giu - sti - zia e di spe -
mf
mon - do sen - za piú vio - len - za. Un mon - do di giu - sti - zia e di spe -
mf
Fsus
F
B♭maj7
Fsus
F
Dm
ran - za. O - gnu - no dia la ma - no al suo vi - ci - no sim - bo - lo di
ran - za. O - gnu - no dia la ma - no al suo vi - ci - no sim - bo - lo di

D♭
B♭m
Fsus
F
cresc.
pa - ce, di tra - ter - ni - tá.
cresc.
pa - ce, di tra - ter - ni - tá.
La for - za che ci
cresc.
Verse 3:
E♭
Fsus
F
Fsus
F
B♭
We ask that life be kind,
and watch us from a -
dai
é il de - si - de - rio che.
B♭(9)/D
E♭
Fsus
F
bove.
We hope each soul will find
O - gnu - no tro - vi a - more
in - tor - no e den - tro

A♭/B♭
B♭
mf
an - oth - er soul to love. Let this be our
sé. Let this be our
dim.
Chorus:
Cm
Cm7/F
F7
F7/E♭
D7sus
prayer, let this be our prayer, just like ev - 'ry
prayer, just like ev - 'ry child,
mf
D7
Gm
E♭
Gm
Dm
mp
child, need to find a place, guide us with your grace.
need to find a place, guide us with your grace.
dim.

E♭
B♭/F
F7
E♭/B♭
B♭
B♭/A
cresc.
Give us faith so we'll be safe.
cresc.
Give us faith so we'll be safe.
cresc.
Freely
Gm
E♭
Gm
Dm
E♭
B♭/F
F7
mf
cresc.
f
mp
molto rit.
E la fe - de che hai a - cce - so in noi. Sen - to che ci sal - ve -
mf
cresc.
f
mp
molto rit.
E la fe - de che hai a - cce - so in noi. Sen - to che ci sal - ve -
mf
cresc.
f
mp
molto rit.
G♭
A♭
B♭
rá.
rá.
p

SAY YOU'LL BE THERE

Words and Music by
SPICE GIRLS and
ELIOT KENNEDY

E♭
G♭
D♭
that we had this con-ver-sa-tion I de-ci - ded we should be friends, yeah.
B♭m
E♭
G♭
But now we're go-ing round in cir-cles tell me will this dé-jà vu nev-er end
D♭
B♭m
E♭
Oh now you tell me that you've fall-en in love well I nev-
(Verses 2 & 3 see block lyric)
G♭
D♭
B♭m
- er ev - er thought that would be, yeah. This time you

E♭
fr3
G♭
D♭
got - ta take_ it ea - sy throw-ing far too much e - mo- tion at me___ but a - ny fool_
D♭11
G♭maj7
fr4
C♭11
___ can see___ they're fall - ing, I got-ta make you un - der - stand._
To Coda
A♭sus4
fr4
B♭m
E♭
fr3
___ (I'll) I'm giv - ing you eve - ry - thing_ all that joy_
G♭m
D♭
B♭m
___ can bring_ this I swear.___ And all that I want_

E♭
G♭m
from you is a pro - - mise you will be there,
1.
D♭
B♭m
E♭
say you will be there,
oh
say you will be there,
B♭m
E♭
2.
D♭
D.𝄋. al Coda
won't you sing it with me.
⊕ Coda
N.C.
3
3
give you eve-ry-thing on this I swear just pro-mise you'll al-ways be there.

Verse 2:
If you put two and two together you will see what our friendship is for,
If you can't work this equation then I guess I'll have to show you the door,
There is no need to say you love me it would be better left unsaid.

I'm giving you everything all that joy can bring this I swear,
And all that I want from you is a promise you will be there,
Yeah I want you.

Verse 3: (Instrumental)
Any fool can see they're falling, gotta make you understand.
To Coda

SMOOTH

Music and Lyrics by
ITAAL SHUR and ROB THOMAS

Dm7 F/C Bm7(♭5) E7/G♯ Am F E7
words melt ev - 'ry one. But you stay so cool.
Am F E7
My mu - ñe - qui - ta, my Span - ish Har - lem Mo - na
Am F E7 Dm7 F/C Bm7(♭5)
Lis - a. You're my rea - son for rea - son,
E7/G♯ Am F E7
the step in my groove. And if you said

Pre-Chorus:
Am
F
E7
this life ain't good e - nough, I would give my world to
3. (Inst. solo ad lib....
lift you up. I could change my life to bet - ter suit your mood.
Dm7
F/C
G7/B
G7
F♯7sus
'Cause you're so smooth.
Chorus:
...end solo) Oh, and it's just like the o - cean un - der the moon. Well, it's the

Am
F
E7
Am
F
E7
same as the e - mo - tion that I get from you.___ You got the kind of lov - ing that can
To Coda ⊕
1.
Dm7
E7(♯5)
N.C.
be so smooth,_ yeah. Give me your heart,_ make it real___ or else for - get a - bout it.
Am
F
E7
Am
F
E7
2.
N.C.
D.S. 𝄋 al Coda
2. Well, I'll tell you ___ or else for - get a - bout it.

Verse 2:
Well, I'll tell you one thing,
If you would leave, it be a crying shame.
In every breath and every word
I hear your name calling me out, yeah.
Well, out from the barrio,
You hear my rhythm on your radio.
You feel the tugging of the world,
So soft and slow, turning you 'round and 'round.
(To Pre-Chorus:)

SHE'S ALL I EVER HAD

Words and Music by
ROBI ROSA, GEORGE NORIEGA
and JON SECADA

Here I am, a - lone a - gain.
It's the way she cared, the love we shared.
I need her now to hold my hand. She's
And through it all, she's al - ways been there. She's
Pre-chorus:
G♯m7
F♯
all, she's all I ev - er
all, she's all I ev - er
all, she's all I ev - er
E(9)
F♯
had. She's the air I breathe. She's
had. In a world so cold, so emp - ty, she's
had. I have to make her see, yeah. She's

G♯m7
F♯
all,
she's all I ev - er had.
all,
she's all I ev - er had.
all,
she's all I ev - er had.
E(9)
Em6
Chorus:
B
F♯/B
It's the way she makes me feel,
it's the on - ly thing that's real.
E
Em6
It's the way she un - der - stands,
she's my lov - er, she's my friend.

B
F♯/B
And when I look in - to her eyes, it's the way I feel in - side,
E
To Coda
Em6
like the man I want to be. She's all I'll ev - er need.
B(9)
4
1.
2.

D.S. 𝄋 al Coda
She's
𝄌 Coda
Em6
B
She's all I'll ev - er need.
It's the way she makes me feel,
F♯/B
E
it's the on - ly thing that's real.
It's the way she un - der - stands,
Em6
B
she's my lov - er, she's my friend.
And when I look in - to her eyes,

F♯/B
E
it's the way I feel inside,
like the man I want to be.
Em6
B(9)
She's all I'll ev-er need.
Here I am.

SHOW ME THE WAY

Lyrics and Music by
DENNIS DE YOUNG

G♭ A♭m7 D♭/F E♭m C♭ D♭sus D♭
feel this emp - ty place in - side; so a - fraid that I've lost my faith. Show me the
mf
Chorus:
G♭ D♭ C♭ G♭ D♭ C♭
way, show me the way.
Take me to -
Bring me to -
f
To Coda
G♭ D♭/F E♭m7 G♭/D♭ A♭m7 D♭sus D♭
night to the riv - er and wash my il - lu - sions a - way.
night to the moun-tain and take my con - fu - sion a - way.
Please show me the
1. D.S. 2.
G♭ C♭/G♭ D♭/G♭ C♭/G♭ G♭ C♭/G♭ D♭/G♭ C♭/G♭ G♭ C♭/G♭ D♭/G♭ C♭
way. 2. And
Bridge:
B♭ E♭m
and if I see a light, should I be - lieve? Tell me, how will I

A♭7
A♭m7
D♭sus
D♭
D♭sus
D♭
A
B/A
Amaj7
B/A
know?
D.S.S. al Coda
A
B/A
A
B/A
Amaj7
B/A
D♭
C♭/D♭
D♭
C♭/D♭
Show me the
Coda
G♭
D♭
C♭
G♭
D♭
C♭
way,
show me the
way.
Take me to -
G♭
D♭/F
E♭m7
G♭/D♭
A♭m7
D♭sus
D♭
night to the riv - er and wash my il - lu - sions a - way.
Show me the
G♭
D♭
C♭
G♭
D♭
C♭
way,
show me the
way.
Give me the

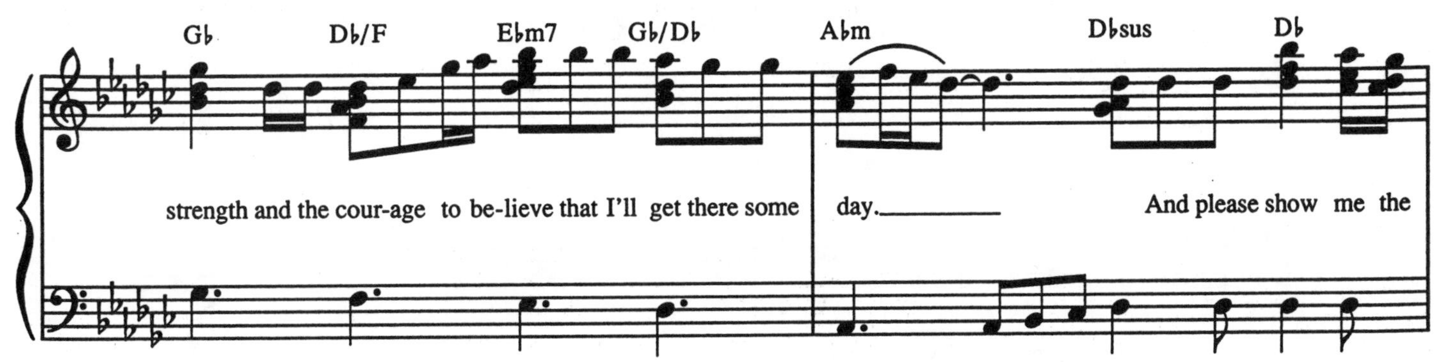

Verse 2:
And as I slowly drift to sleep
For a moment dreams are sacred.
I close my eyes and know there's peace
In a world so filled with hatred.
Then I wake up each morning and turn on the news
To find we've so far to go.
And I keep on hoping for a sign
So afraid I just won't know.
(To Chorus:)

THE WAY SHE LOVES ME

Words and Music by
RICHARD MARX

𝄋

Db

Verse:

1. I'll have this feel - ing ’till the day that I die, when I hear my ba - by call - in'.

2. Came close to let - ting this train pass me by, just like a fool sec - ond guess - in'.

3. *(Instrumental solo ad lib....*

Cb

Db

A sim - ple mo - tion, a look in her eyes and I'm help - less - ly fall - in'.

I could have spent my life won - der - ing why I did - n't cher - ish the bless - ing.

...end solo)

Ebm7

Ab

I'd give all of some - bod - y else

If I'd have known she'd come my way

No - bod - y else could do me so right,

Db
Gb
for an - y piece of her heart___ that's left.___
the lone - ly nights would - 've been___ o - kay.___
a breath of heav - en in my dark - est night.___
Ebm7
Absus
Ab
She knows me bet - ter than I know my - self.___
I have her prom - ise that she's gon - na stay.___
I'm gon - na hold on with all of my might.___
Chorus:
E
F#m7
Let me tell you 'bout the way she loves_ me. Ooh,___ I want the world to know._
E
I'm cra - zy 'bout the way she loves_ me. Ooh,_
F#m7
1. 2.
D.S.
3.
Repeat ad lib. and fade
___ I'm proud to let it show.___

From the Motion Picture "SOMETHING TO TALK ABOUT"

SOMETHING TO TALK ABOUT

Words and Music by
SHIRLEY EIKHARD

Something to Talk About - 5 - 1

Db/Ab
Ab
4 fr.
4fr.
People are talking, talking 'bout people.
I feel so foolish, I never noticed.
I hear them whisper, you won't believe it.
You'd act so nervous, could you be falling for me?
Db
Gb/Db
They think we're lovers kept under covers.
It took a rumour to make me wonder.
I just ignore it, but they keep saying... We
Now I'm convinced I'm going under.

Fm7
Gb(addAb)
Fm7
laugh just a lit-tle too loud,
Think-ing 'bout you ev-er-y day,
stand just a lit-tle too close,
dream-ing 'bout you ev-er-y night,
Gb(addAb)
Cb
Fb
we stare just a lit-tle too long.
hop-ing that you feel the same way.
Eb7
May-be they're see-ing some-thing we don't, dar-lin'.
Now that we know it let's real-ly show it, dar-lin'.
Ab
Ab7/C
Eb7
4fr.
Let's give them some-thing to talk a-bout.
Let's give them some-thing to talk
A lit-tle mys-tery to fig-

Ab 4fr. | Ab7/C | Eb7 | Fm7

a - bout.
ure out.

Let's give them some-thing to talk a - bout. How a - bout love?

Gb6/9 | Db 4fr. | 1. Fb | Ab 4fr. | 2. Fb | Ab 4fr.

Ab 4fr. | Ab7/C | Eb7 | Ab 4fr. | Ab7/C | Eb7

Ab 4fr. | Ab7/C | Eb7 | Fm7

B
No Chord
Let's give them some-thing to talk a-bout, babe,
a lit-tle mys-tery to fig-ure out.
B
B7/D♯
F♯7
Let's give them some-thing to talk
G♯m7
4fr.
A6/9
E
G
a-bout. How a-bout love?
Repeat and fade
B
B7/D♯
F♯7
B
B7/D♯
F♯7
B
B7/D
F♯7
G♯m7
4fr.
A6/9
E
G

SOMEDAY

Words and Music by
SUGAR RAY and DAVID KAHNE

Someday - 6 - 1

F♯m E F♯m

I'll lay a-round and won-der why__ you were al-ways there__ for me.__
No mat-ter what they try to say,__ you were al-ways there__ for me.__

E F♯m E

One way,
Some way,

F♯m E F♯m

in the eyes of a pass-er-by,__ I'll look a-round for an-
when the sun__ be-gins to shine,__ I hear a song from an-

E F♯m 1. E F♯m *To Next Strain*

oth-er try__ and fade a-way.
oth-er time__ and fade a-

2.
E
F♯m
E
F♯m
way, and fade a - way.
Chorus:
A
G♯m
A
Just close your eyes and I'll take you there. This place is warm with -
G♯m
A
G♯m
out a care. We'll take a swim in the deep blue sea.
F♯m
1.
D.S.𝄋
2.
B
B
I go to leave as you reach for me. reach for me.

E
F♯m11
E
F♯m11
Oh.
Come on.
E
F♯m
Some-one said you tried too long.
(So long, we'll pass me by.)
Some-one said we
E
got it all wrong.
(Some - day I'll won - der.)
Some-one said we tried too long.
(So long, we'll
F♯m
E
pass me by.)
Ev - 'ry-thing's where I be - long.
(So long, I'm gone.)
So far, and

F♯m
E
so long.
So far a - way.
E
F♯m
E
F♯m
So far,
so wrong.
So far a - way, a - way, a - way.
Verse 3:
E
F♯m11
E
3. Some - day, when my life has passed me by,
F♯m11
E
F♯m11
I'll lay a - round and won - der why you were al - ways there for me.

E
F♯m11
One way,
(Some-one said you
tried, oh.
in the eyes of a pass-er - by,
In the eyes of a pass-er - by.
I look a-round for an - oth-er try
Look a-round for an - oth-er try.)
and fade a - way,
(And fade a - way.)
and fade a - way.
(And fade a - way.)
And fade a -
Repeat ad lib. and fade

SOMETHING ABOUT THE WAY YOU LOOK TONIGHT

Lyrics by
BERNIE TAUPIN

Music by
ELTON JOHN

F♯ A♯m7

Oh I need to tell— you how you light up ev - ery sec - ond of the day,—
smile— you pull the deep - est sec - rets from my heart.

D♯m F♯/C♯ B

but in the moon - light— you just
In all hon - est - y— I'm

G♯m7 C♯

shine like a bea - con on— the bay.— And I can't ex -
speech - less and I don't know where to start.—

F♯ A♯7 D♯m

-plain— but it's some - thing a - bout— the way— you look to - night.

D#7
G#m
G#m7
It takes my breath a - way.
It's that feel-ing I get a- bout you
C#
F#
deep in - side.
And I can't des- cribe
but it's
A#7
D#m
F#/C#
B
F#/A#
G#m
F#
fr 3
some-thing a - bout the way you look to - night.
It takes my breath a - way,
C#
1.
F#
C#
the way you look to - night.
With your

2.
F♯
A
B
fr 4
night.
The way you look to - night.
The way you
look to - night.
The way you look to - night.
The way you
look to-night.
The way you look
to-night.
The way you look to-night.
The way you look to-night.
The way you look
to - night.

LOVE WILL KEEP US ALIVE

Words and Music by
JIM CAPALDI, PETER VALE
and PAUL CARRACK

D2(6)
You were search - ing
The world is chang - ing
When we're hun - gry
for a place to hide.
right be - fore your eyes.
love will keep us a -
Esus
E
A2
live.
Lost and lone - ly,
Now I've found you,
(Instrumental solo . . .
F♯m11
now you've giv - en me the will to sur - vive.
there's no more emp - ti - ness in - side.
When we're
When we're

To Coda
1.
D2(6)
Esus
E
A2
hun - gry, love will keep us a - live.
hun - gry, love will keep us a - live.
2.3.
A2
2. Don't you
... end solo)
I would
Bridge:
D
F♯m7
die for you,
climb the high - est moun -

Bm7
tain.
Ba - by,
there's noth-ing I
would-n't
E
E/D
1.
D.S.
C♯m7
E/B
2.
D.S. al Coda
C♯m7
E/B
do.
3. Now, I've
4. I was
Coda
A2
F♯m11
When we're

D2(6)
Esus
E
A2
hun - gry,
love will keep us a - live.
F#m11
D2(6)
Esus
When we're hun - gry,
love will keep us a - live.
A2
rit.

STRONG ENOUGH

Words and Music by
MARK TAYLOR and
PAUL BARRY

Cm7
Fm7
Fm7/B♭
And I hear your reasons why.
Where did you sleep
E♭
Cm7
Fm7
last night?
And was she worth it?
Was
Fm7/B♭
Gsus
Gm7/C
she worth it?
'Cause I'm strong
𝄋 Chorus:
Dm7
Gm7
Gm7/C
enough to live without you, strong enough.
And I

F Dm7 Gm7

quit cry - ing long e-nough, now I'm strong e - nough to know

Gm7/C Asus Dm7

you've got - ta go. {There's no more to say, so save
(*Inst. solo ad lib....*)

Gm7 Gm7/C F

your breath and walk a - way. No mat - ter what I hear

Dm7 Gm7 Gm7/C *To Coda* ⊕

you say, I'm strong e - nough to know you've

Verse 2:
Asus
Dm7
Gm7
3
got - ta go. 2. So you feel mis - un - der-stood?
Gm7/C
F
Dm7
Ba - by, have I got news for you. On be - ing used, I could write
Gm7
3
Gm7/C
F
the book. But you don't wan - na hear a - bout it.
Dm7
Gm7
3
Gm7/C
'Cause I've been los - ing sleep, and you've been go -

F
Dm7
Gm7
in' cheap.
And she ain't worth half of me, it's true.
Gm7/C
Asus
D.S. 𝄋 al Coda
Now, I'm tell - ing you that I'm strong
Coda
Asus
Verse 3:
Dm7
Gm7
... end solo)
Come hell or wa - ters high,
Gm7/C
F
Dm7
you'll nev - er see me cry.
This is our last good -

Gm7
Gm7/C
Am7/D
bye, it's true. I'm tell - ing you, 'cause I'm strong
Chorus:
Em7
Am7
Am7/D
e - nough to live with - out you, strong e - nough. And I
G
Em7
Am7
quit cry - ing long e - nough, now I'm strong e - nough to know
Am7/D
Bsus
Em7
you've got - ta go. There's no more to say, so save

Am7
Am7/D
G
your breath and walk a - way. No mat - ter what I hear
Em7
Am7
you say, I'm strong e - nough to know
Am7/D
Bsus
Repeat ad lib. and fade
you've got - ta go. 'Cause I'm strong

THE SWEETEST DAYS

Words and Music by
WENDY WALDMAN, JON LIND
and PHIL GALDSTON

E♭
B♭/F
F
E♭
out - side the thun - der rolls.
bat - tle the fear we feel.
Lis - ten now,
All the while
B♭/D
D/F♯
you can hear our heart - beat,
life is rush - ing by us.
warm a - gainst life's bit - ter cold.
Hold it now and don't let go.
Gm
E♭
Cm7(4)
F7sus
These are the days, the sweet - est days we'll know.
These are the days, the sweet - est days we'll know.
1.
B♭
F/A
Gm
E♭
B♭
F
E♭

2.
Bridge:
B♭sus
B♭
B♭sus
B♭
B♭/D
E♭
So we'll whis-per our dreams_
mf
Gm
F
B♭/D
E♭
F7sus
F
here in the dark - ness,
watch-ing the stars_
till they're gone._
And when
B♭/D
E♭
F
D/F♯
Gm
Cm7
F7sus
F
e-ven the mem-'ries have all
fad-ed a - way,_
these days go on___
and___ on._
E♭
B♭/D
D/F♯
Lis-ten now,
you can hear_ our heart - beat.
Hold me now and don't_ let go._
mp

Gm
E♭
Cm7(4)
F7sus
Gm
(These are the days.) Ev-'ry day is the sweet - est day we'll know;
(These are the days.
mf
E♭
Cm7(4)
F7sus
B♭
F/A
the sweet - est days we'll know.
)
mp
Gm
E♭
B♭
F
E♭2
poco rit. e dim. p

TEARS IN HEAVEN

Words and Music by
WILL JENNINGS and ERIC CLAPTON

C♯/E♯
A7/E
F♯
E/G♯
F♯7/A♯
and car - ry on,
through night and day,
'cause I know
'cause I know
Bm7
E7sus
A
E/G♯
F♯m
I don't be - long
I just can't stay
here in heav - en.
here in heav - en.
A/E
D/F♯
E7sus
E7
1.
A
2.
A
Bridge:
C
Bm7
Am7
D/F♯
Time can bring you down,
time can bend your knees.

G
D/F♯
Em7
D/F♯
G
C
Bm7
Time can break your heart,
Am7
D/F♯
G
D/F♯
E
A/E
E7
have you beg - ging, "Please!"
Beg-ging, "Please!"
Verse:
A
E/G♯
F♯m
A/E
D/F♯
A/E
(Instrmental solo . . .
Would you know my name
if I saw you in heav -
E
A/E
E7
A
E/G♯
F♯m
A/E
en?
Would you be the same

D/F♯
A/E
E
A/E
E7
F♯m
. . . end solo)
if I saw you in heav - en?
Be-yond the door,
I must be strong
C♯/E♯
A7/E
F♯
E/G♯
F♯7/A♯
Bm7
there's peace I'm sure.
and car - ry on,
And I know
'cause I know
there'll be no more
I don't be-long
E7sus
A
E/G♯
F♯m
A/E
tears in heav - en.
here in heav - en.
1.
D/F♯
E7sus
E7
A
2.
D/F♯
E7sus
E7
A
molto rit.

TELL HIM

Words and Music by
LINDA THOMPSON, DAVID FOSTER
and WALTER AFANASIEFF

D♯/F𝄪
G♯m
Ooh, what if there's an-oth - er one he's
2. See additional lyrics
mf
D♯m/F♯
Emaj7
F♯/E
think-ing of? May - be he's in love. I'd feel like a
D♯m7
G♯m7
C♯m7
B
fool. Life can be so cruel. I don't know what to do.
Emaj7
Barbra:
I've been there, with my heart out in my

D#m7
G#m7
D
hand. But what you must un - der - stand, you can't let the
A/C#
E
chance to love him pass you by.
Chorus:
A
F#m7
Both:
Tell him, tell him that the sun and moon rise
D6
Bm7(b5)/E
E
A
in his eyes. Reach out to him and whis - per

F♯m7
Dmaj7
Celine:
ten - der words so soft and sweet. I'll hold him close to feel his heart beat.
1.
Bm7/E
E
A
Barbra:
Love will be the gift you give your - self.
2.
Bm7/E
A
Celine:
Love will be the gift you give your - self.
Bridge:
F
B♭maj7
Em7
C/E
Dm7
G7/B
Love is light that sure - ly glows in the hearts of those who know. It's a stead - y flame that

C
A♭
D♭maj7
Cm7
Fm7
Barbra:
Celine:
grows.
Feed the fire with all the pas - sion
you can show.
To - night,
B♭m7
A♭/C
D♭maj7
E♭/F
Fm7
Barbra:
love will
as - sume
it's
place.
This
mem - 'ry
time
can - not
e - rase.
B♭m7
A♭/C
Fsus
F
Both:
Your
faith
will lead love
where it
has
to
go.
rall.
B♭
Gm7
E♭6
Tell
him,
tell
him
that the sun
and moon rise
in his eyes.
Reach
a tempo

Verse 2:
(Barbra:)
Touch him with the gentleness you feel inside. (*C:* I feel it.)
Your love can't be denied.
The truth will set you free.
You'll have what's meant to be.
All in time, you'll see.
(Celine:)
I love him, *(B:* Then show him.*)*
Of that much I can be sure. *(B:* Hold him close to you.)
I don't think I could endure
If I let him walk away
When I have so much to say.
(To Chorus:)

THANK U

Words by
ALANIS MORISSETTE

Music by
ALANIS MORISSETTE
and GLEN BALLARD

Cmaj7(no3rd) G(add2)

How 'bout them trans - par - ent dan - gl - ing car - rots.
How 'bout how good it feels to fin - 'lly for - give ___ you.

Gsus2/F Cmaj7(no3rd)

How 'bout that ev - er ___ e - lu - sive ku -
How 'bout griev - ing it all one at ___ a ___

G(add2) Gsus2/F Cmaj7(no3rd)

- do.
___ time.

Thank _ you, In - di - a. ___ Thank you, ter -

G(add2) Gsus2/F

- ror. ___ Thank you, dis - il - lu - sion - ment. ___ Thank you, frail -

Cmaj7(no3rd)
3fr
G(add2)
To Coda
ty. Thank you, con - se-quence. Thank you, thank you, si - lence.
Gsus2/F
Cmaj7(no3rd)
3fr
How 'bout me not blam - ing you for ev - 'ry -
G(add2)
Gsus2/F
Cmaj7(no3rd)
3fr
- thing. How 'bout me en - joy -
G(add2)
Gsus2/F
D.S. al Coda
- ing the mo - ment for once.

CODA
Gsus2/F
Cmaj7(no3rd)
3fr
The mo - ment I let go of it was the mo -
G(add2)
Gsus2/F
Cmaj7(no3rd)
3fr
- ment I got more than I could han - dle. The mo - ment I jumped off
G(add2)
Gsus2/F
of it was the mo - ment I touched down.
Cmaj7(no3rd)
3fr
G(add2)
How 'bout no long - er be - ing mas - o - chis - tic.

Gsus2/F
Cmaj7(no3rd)
3 fr
How 'bout re - mem - ber - ing your di - vin - i - ty.
G(add2)
Gsus2/F
Cmaj7(no3rd)
3 fr
How 'bout un - a - bash -
G(add2)
G7/F
- ed - ly bawl - ing your eyes out.
Cmaj7(no3rd)
3 fr
G(add2)
How 'bout not e - quat - ing death with stop - ping.

Gsus2/F
Cmaj7(no3rd)
3fr
Thank you, India.
Thank you, providence.
Thank you, dis-
G(add2)
Gsus2/F
Cmaj7(no3rd)
illusionment.
Thank you, nothingness.
Thank you, clar-
ity.
G(add2)
Gsus2/F
Thank you, thank you, silence.
A yeah, yeah.
Cmaj7(no3rd)
G(add2)
Gsus2/F
Repeat and Fade
Optional Ending
C5
Ho hey oh hey oh.
Vocal ad lib.

From the Twentieth Century Fox Motion Picture

THAT THING YOU DO!

Words and Music by
ADAM SCHLESINGER

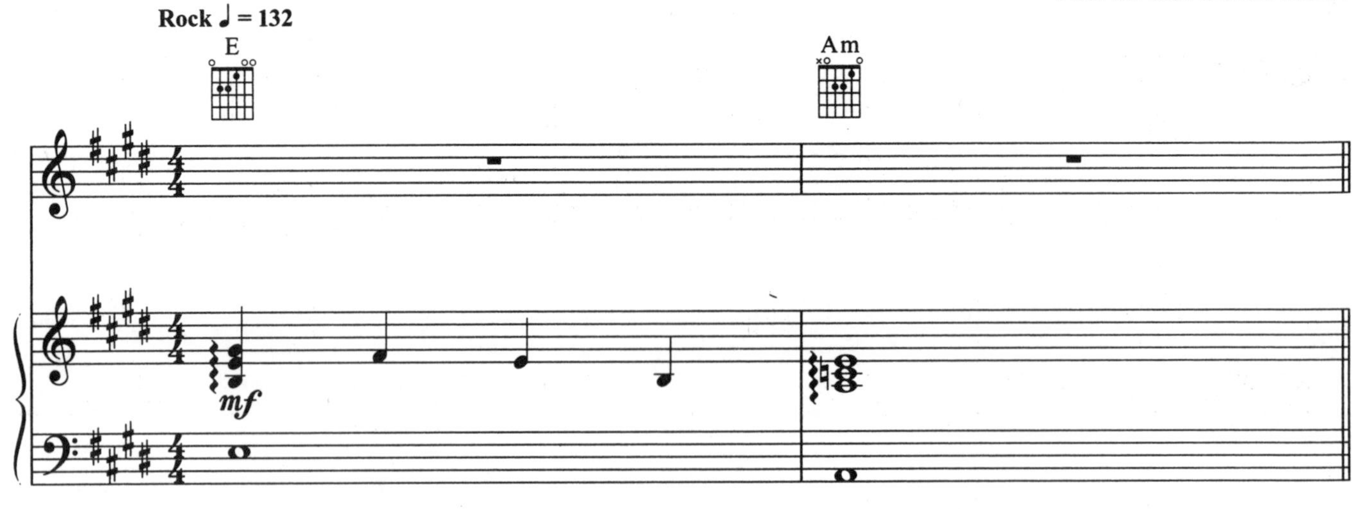

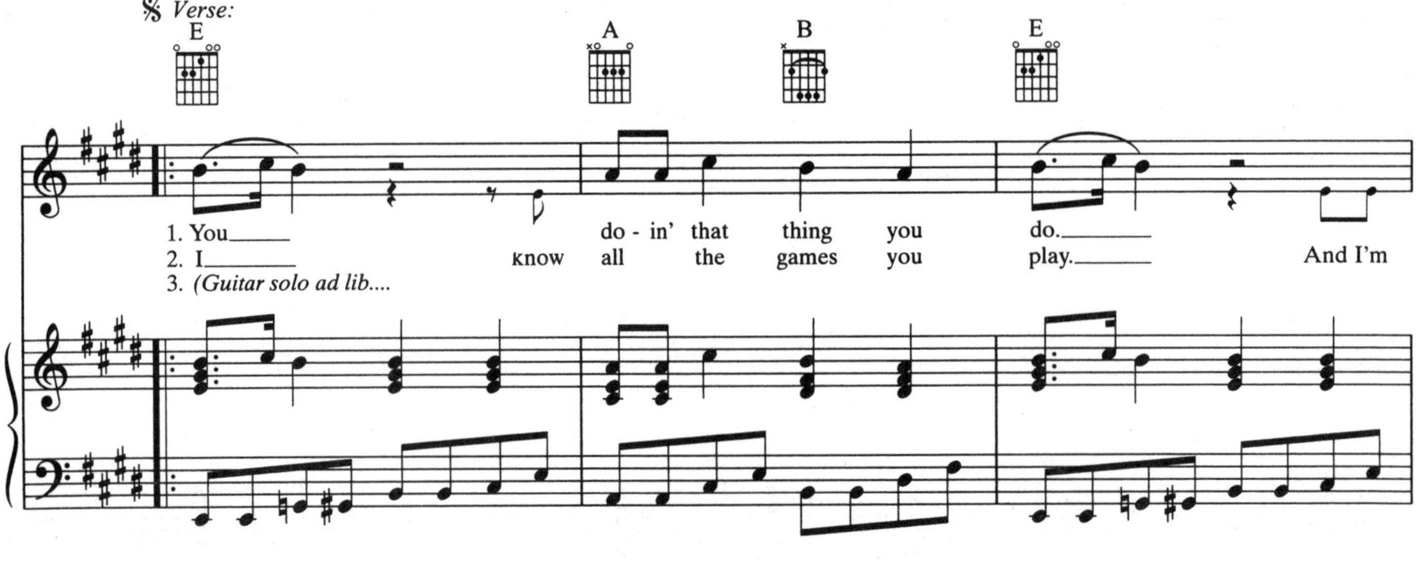

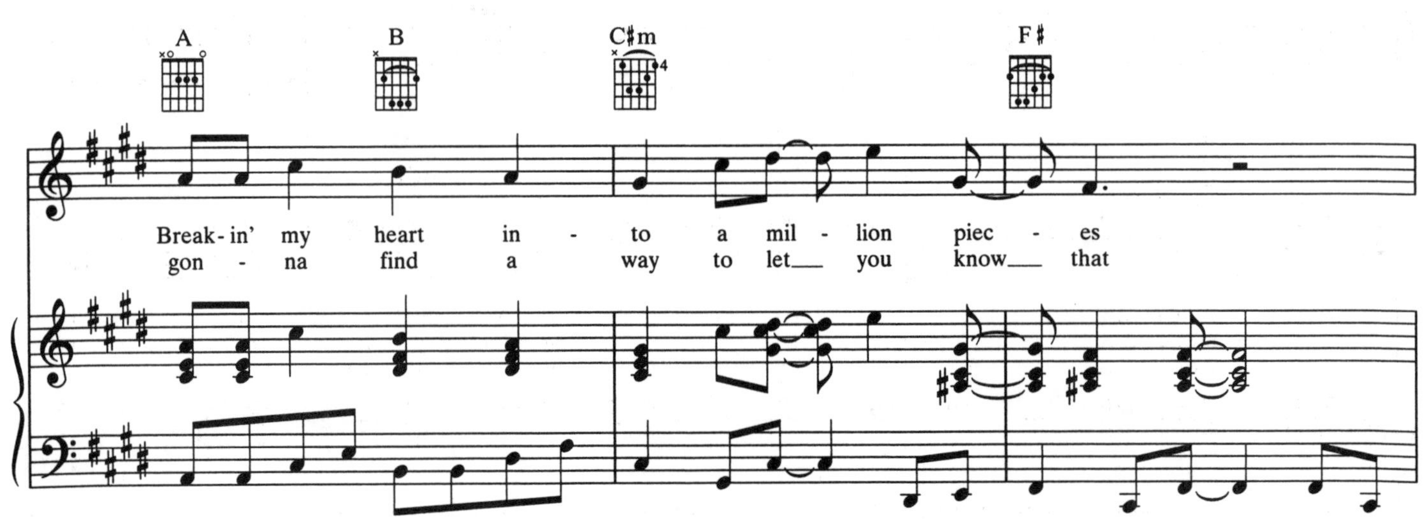

F♯m
Am
B
E
like you al - ways do.
And you
you'll be mine some - day.
'Cause we
could be
... end solo)
'Cause we
could be
A
B
E
A
B
don't mean to be cruel.
You nev - er e - ven
hap - py, can't you see?
If you'd on - ly let me
hap - py, can't you see?
If you'd on - ly let me
C♯m
F♯
D
knew a - bout the heart - ache
I've been go - in'
be the one to hold you
and keep you here with
be the one to hold you
and keep you here with
B
C♯m
F♯
through.
Well, I try and try to for - get you, girl but it's
me.
'Cause I try and try to for - get you, girl but it's
me.
'Cause it hurts me so just to see you go a -

E
E7
A
Am
To Coda
E
just so hard to do. Ev - 'ry time you
just too hard to do. Ev - 'ry time you
round with some - one new. And if
Am
E
1.
B7
2.
do that thing you do.
do that thing you do.
Bridge:
A
C♯m
I don't ask a - lot, girl but I know one thing's for sure
(I don't ask a - lot girl
F♯
It's your love I have - n't got, girl and I
know one thing's for sure.)

B7
C7
B7
D.S. 𝄋 al Coda
just can't take it an - y - more,
wow.
Coda
E
Am
E
I know you, you're do - in' that thing. Ev - 'ry day just
Am
E
B7
do - in' that thing.
I can't take you do - in' that thing you do.
A
Am
E
Emaj7

THAT'S THE WAY IT IS

Words and Music by
MAX MARTIN, KRISTIAN LUNDIN
and ANDREAS CARLSSON

C♯m
A
B
see what you're go - ing through, yeah. It's an
I don't know what to say, no. But it's
C♯m
A
up - hill climb and I'm feel - ing sor - ry, but I
plain to see, if you stick to - geth - er,
C♯m
B
E
know it will come to you, yeah.
you're gon - na find the way, yeah.
Don't sur -
Pre-chorus:
F♯m
A
B
F♯m
ren - der, 'cause you can win in this thing called love.

Chorus:
A
B
E
A
C♯m
B
When you want it the most, there's no eas - y way out. When you're
E
A
C♯m
B
read - y to go and your heart's left in doubt, don't give
E
A
C♯m
B
up on your faith; love comes to those who be - lieve
F♯m
A
B
1.
E5
it, and that's the way it is.
2. When you

2.
E
A
C♯m
B
F♯m
That's the way it is.
Bridge:
A
B
Em
Em/D
When life is emp - ty, with no to - mor - row, and
C
G
D/F♯
Em
lon - li - ness starts to call, ba - by, don't wor - ry, for -
C♯m7(♭5)
C
Dsus
D
E5
get your sor - row, 'cause love's gon - na con - quer it all. Oh. When you

Chorus:
A D F♯m E
want it the most, there's no eas - y way out. When you're
2. Vocal ad lib.
A D F♯m E
read - y to go and your heart's left in doubt, don't give
A D F♯m E
up on your faith; love comes to those who be - lieve
Bm
1.
D E
it, and that's the way it is.

2.
D
E
A
D
that's the way it is.
That's the way it is.
F♯m
E
A
D
F♯m
E
(That's the way it is.)
That's the way it is.
(That's the way it is.)
Don't give
A
D
F♯m
E
up on your faith;
love comes to those who be - lieve
Bm
D
E
A
it,
and that's the way it is.
rit.

THINK TWICE

Words and Music by
ANDY HILL and PETE SINFIELD

Gm
C
Am7
B♭
dis - tant light,
and you and I
know there'll be a storm to - night.
Gm7
This is get - ting ser - i - ous.
Are you think-ing 'bout
cresc.
𝄋𝄋 Chorus:
F
you or us? 1.-3.5. Don't say what you're a - bout to say.
4. See additional lyrics
Look back
mf
Am
be - fore you leave my life.
Be sure be - fore you close that door,

C
Gm7
before you roll those dice,
1.
B♭
F
Gm
D.S. 𝄋
baby, think twice.
2. Baby, think
2.
B♭
To Next Strain
3.4.etc.
B♭
Repeat ad lib. and fade
Dm
baby, think
4. Don't do twice.
5. Don't say
(Instrumental solo . . .
Gm
Dm
Gm
. . . end solo)

Verse 2:
Baby, think twice for the sake of our love, for the memory,
For the fire and the faith that was you and me.
Baby, I know it ain't easy when your soul cries out for higher ground,
'Cos when you're halfway up, you're always halfway down.
But baby, this is serious.
Are you thinking 'bout you or us?
(To Chorus:)

Chorus 4:
Don't do what you're about to do.
My everything depends on you,
And whatever it takes, I'll sacrifice.
Before you roll those dice,
Baby, think twice.

UN-BREAK MY HEART

Words and Music by
DIANE WARREN

Bm
Em7
A
F♯7
Come back and bring back my smile, come and take these tears a - way. I
Don't leave me here with these tears, come and kiss this pain a - way. I
Bm
Em7
A
need your arms to hold me now. Nights are so un - kind.
can't for - get the day you left. Time is so un - kind,
Bm
Em7
A
A7
Bring back those nights when I held you be - side me.
and life is so cruel with - out you here be - side me.
Un - break my heart,
Chorus:
Dm
Gm7
C
A7
say you love me a - gain. Un - do this hurt

Dm
Gm7
C
A7
_ you caused_ when you walked_ out the door_ and walked out___ of my life._ Un - cry_ these tears_
To Coda
Dm
Gm7
C
A7
___ I cried so man - y nights.___ Un - break_ my heart._
1.
2.
C/B♭
B♭
A7
F♯7
D♯
G♯m
C♯m7
F♯
D♯m7

G♯m
C♯m7
F♯7
Bridge:
Bm
Em7
A
Don't leave me in all this pain,
don't leave me out in the rain.
Bm
Em7
A
D.S. 𝄋 ál Coda
Bring back those nights when I held you be - side me.
Un - break my heart,
Coda
C
A7
Dm
Gm7
Un - break my, un - break my heart, sweet ba - by.

C
A7
Dm
Gm7
Come back_ and say_ you love_ me.
Un - break_ my heart,_ sweet dar - ling.
With - out_ you, I_ just can't_ go_ on._
Repeat ad lib. and fade

WAITING FOR TONIGHT

Words and Music by MICHAEL GARVIN,
MARIA CHRISTENSEN and PHIL TEMPLE

Verse:
B♭m
A♭6
Fm7
1. Like a mov - ie scene,_ in the sweet-est dreams,_ I have pic-tured us to -
2. Ten - der words you say___ take my breath a - way.___ Love me now and leave me
G♭maj7
B♭m
A♭6
geth - er.________ Now to feel__ your lips__ on my fin - ger - tips,__
nev - er.________ Found a sa - cred place,_ lost in your__ em - brace._
Fm7
G♭maj7
B♭m
I have to say__ is e - ven bet - ter________ than I ev - er thought it____ could
I want to stay__ in this for - ev - er.________ I (2.3.) think of__ the days when_ the
A♭6
Fm7
G♭maj7
pos - si - bly be. It's per - fect,_ it's pas - sion,_ it's set - ting_ me free from
sun used__ to set on my emp - ty heart, all___ a - lone in___ my bed.

B♭m
A♭6
Fm7
all of my sad - ness, the tears that I've cried. I have spent all of my
Toss - ing and turn - ing, e - mo - tions were strong. I knew I had to hold
Chorus:
G♭maj7
B♭m
A♭6
life
on,
wait-ing for to - night, oh, when
Fm7
G♭maj7
B♭m
you would be here in my arms. Wait-ing for to - night, oh.
To Coda
A♭6
Fm7
G♭maj7
I've dreamed of this love for so long. Wait-ing for to -

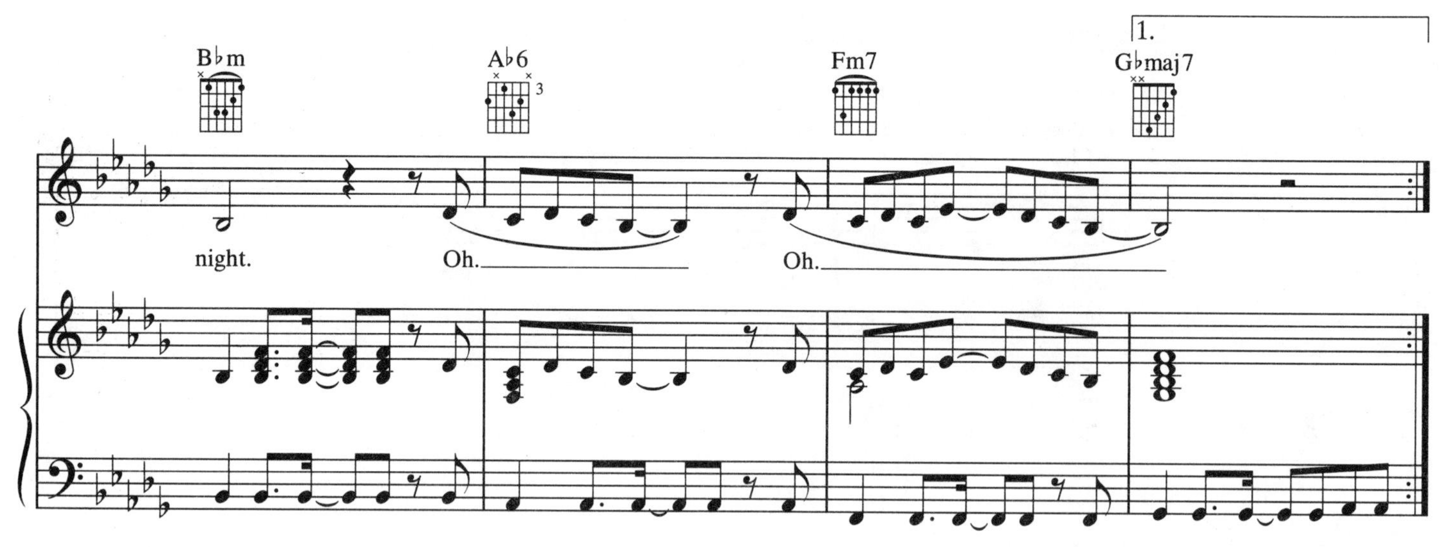
1.
B♭m
A♭6
Fm7
G♭maj7
night.
Oh.
Oh.

2.
G♭maj7
B♭m
A♭6
Oh.
Oh.
Oh.

Fm7
1.2.
G♭maj7
3.
G♭maj7
D.S. 𝄋 al Coda
Oh.
I

Coda
G♭maj7
B♭m
A♭6
long. Wait-ing for to - night, oh, when
Fm7
G♭maj7
B♭m
you would be here in my arms. Wait-ing for to - night, oh.
A♭6
Fm7
1.2.3.
G♭maj7
I've dreamed of this love for so long. Wait-ing for to -
4.
G♭maj7
B♭m
long. Wait - ing for to - night, oh.

VALENTINE

Composed by
JIM BRICKMAN and JACK KUGELL

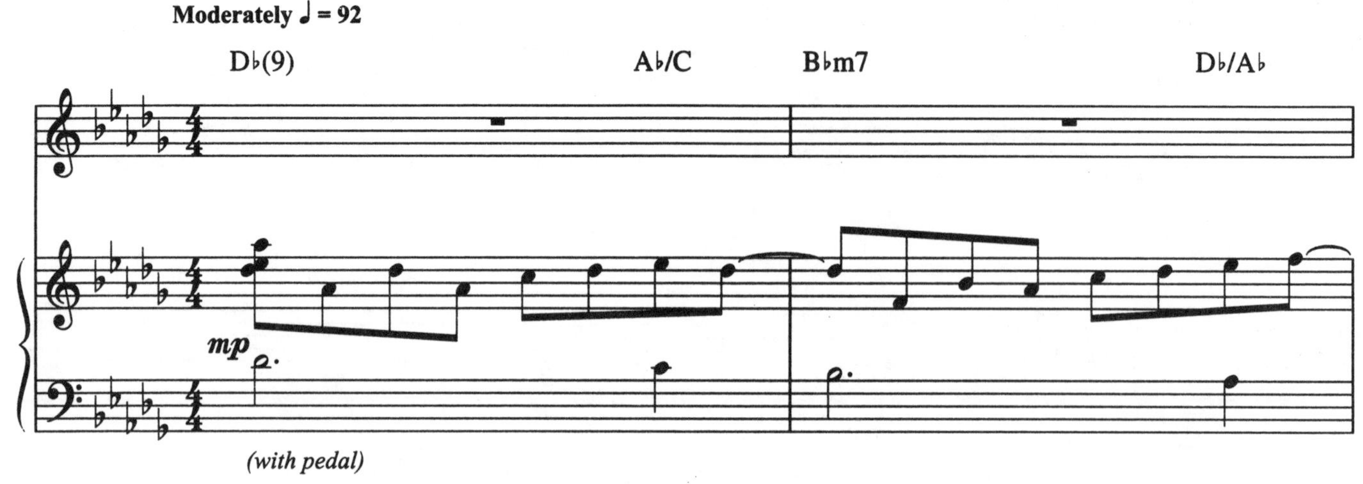

A♭sus A♭ D♭(9) B♭m7
would still hear you. If there were no tears, no way to feel
G♭(9) A♭7sus D♭(9)/F
in - side, I'd still feel for you. And e - ven if the sun
G♭(9) A♭ Fm7 D♭(9)/F G♭(9) A♭
re - fused to shine, e - ven if ro - mance ran out of rhyme,
E♭m7 F7sus F7 B♭m D♭/A♭
you would still have my heart un - til the end of time.

Gm7(♭5)
D♭/A♭
G♭/A♭
You're all I need, my love, my Val - en - tine.
D♭(9)
A♭/C
B♭m7
D♭/A♭
G♭(9)
G♭/A♭
D♭(9)
B♭m7
G♭(9)
All of my life, I have been wait - ing for all
A♭sus
A♭
D♭(9)
B♭m7
you give to me. You've o - pened my eyes and shown me how

G♭(9)
A♭7sus
A♭
D♭(9)/F
to love un - self - ish - ly. I've dreamed of this a thou-
mf
G♭(9)
A♭
Fm7
D♭(9)/F
G♭(9)
A♭
- sand times be - fore, but in my dreams I could - n't love you more.
E♭m7
F7sus
F7
B♭m
D♭/A♭
I will give you my heart un - til the end of time.
Gm7(♭5)
D♭/A♭
G♭/A♭
You're all I need, my love, my Val - en - tine.

D♭(9) B♭m7 G♭(9) G♭/B♭ A♭/C
D♭(9) B♭m7 G♭(9) D♭/A♭ A♭
And
D♭(9)/F G♭(9) A♭ Fm7 D♭(9)/F
e - ven if the sun re - fused to shine, e - ven if ro - mance
G♭(9) A♭ E♭m7 F7sus F7
ran out of rhyme, you would still have my heart un - til

B♭m
D♭/A♭
Gm7(♭5)
D♭/A♭
the end of time.
'Cause all I need is you,
G♭/A♭
E♭m7
D♭/F
G♭
my Val - en - tine.
You're
mp
D♭/A♭
G♭/A♭
D♭(9)
A♭/C
all I need, my love, my Val - en - tine.
B♭m7
D♭/A♭
G♭(9)
G♭/A♭
D♭(9)
rit. e dim.
p

WALKING IN MEMPHIS

Words and Music by
MARC COHN

*chord symbols in parentheses indicate implied harmony

(Am) (F) (G) (C) (Am) (F)
Del - ta Blues_ in the mid-dle of the pour - ing rain.___
(G) (C) (Am) (F) (G) (C)
W.______ C. Han - dy, won't you look down o - ver me?_
(dou - ble u___)
(Am) (F) (G) (C) (Am) (F)
Yeah,__ I got a first class__ tick - et, but I'm as
Chorus:
(G) C Am F G C
blue as a boy__ can be.____ Then I'm walk-ing in Mem - phis,

**implied harmony with no bass

(G7sus)
(C/G)
(G7sus)
to the gates of Grace - land, then I watched him walk_ right through._
(C/G)
F2
G7sus
C
Am
Now, se - cu - ri - ty, they did not__ see him. They just
F2
G7sus
C
Am
F2
G7sus
hov - ered 'round his___ tomb._ But there's a pret - ty lit - tle thing_ wait -
C
Am
F
N.C.
3
3
C
ing for the King,_ down in the Jun - gle__Room. When I was walk - ing in Mem -

Chorus:
F G C Am F G C
- phis, I was walk-ing with my feet ten feet__ off of Beale.__
Am F G C Am
— Walk-ing in Mem - phis, but do I real - ly
F G C7sus C7 C7sus C7
feel the way_ I feel?___ They've_ got
mp
dim.
mp
Bridge:
C7sus C7 C7sus C7
cat-fish on the ta - ble.__ They've got

C7sus
C7
C7sus
C7
gos - pel in the air.
And Rev - er - end Green
3
Rubato - vocal ad lib.
E7
F7
F♯dim7
be glad to see you when you have - n't got a
Rubato
G7
C/G
G7
N.C.
(F)
(G)
(C)
prayer.
But boy you got a prayer in Mem - phis...
a tempo
a tempo
(Am)
(F)
(G)
(C)
(Am)
(F)
Now,

Verse:
(G) (C) (Am) (F) (G) (C)
Mu - ri - el plays pi - a - no every Fri - day at the Hol - ly - wood.
(Am) (F) (G) (C) (Am) (F)
And they brought me down to see her, and they
(G) (C) (Am) F2 G7sus C
asked me if I would do a lit - tle num -
mf
cresc.
mf
Am7 F2 G7sus C Am7
- ber. And I sang with all my might. She said,

F2
G7sus
C
Am7
F2
3
N.C.
"Tell_ me, are you a Christ - ian, child?"_ And I____ said, "Ma'am, I am______
cresc.
f
cresc.
f
Chorus:
C
F
G
C
Am
to-night." Walk-ing in Mem - phis, I was walk-ing with my
F
G
C
Am
F
G
C
feet ten feet__ off of Beale.__ Walk-ing in Mem - phis,
1.
Am
F
C/E
Dm
C
Am
but do I real - ly feel the way__ I feel?___ Walk - ing in Mem -

2.
F G Csus (G) (C) (Am) (F)
feel the way I feel?
(G) (C) (Am) (F) (G) (C)
Put on my blue
(Am) (F) (G) (C) (Am) (F)
suede shoes and I board-ed the plane. Touched down
(G) (C) (Am) (F) (G) (C)
in the land of the Del - ta Blues in the mid-dle of the pour - ing rain.
dim.

(Am)
(F)
(G)
(C)
Am
Touched down in the land of the Del - ta Blues in the
mp
rit.
mp
rit.
F
G
(F)
(G)
(C)
(Am)
(F)
mid-dle of the pour - ing rain.
a tempo
a tempo
(G)
(C)
(Am)
(F)
(G)
(C)
(Am)
F
G
C
dim. e rit.
p

WHAT A GIRL WANTS

Words and Music by
GUY ROCHE and
SHELLY PEIKEN

Slow, funky groove ♩ = 72

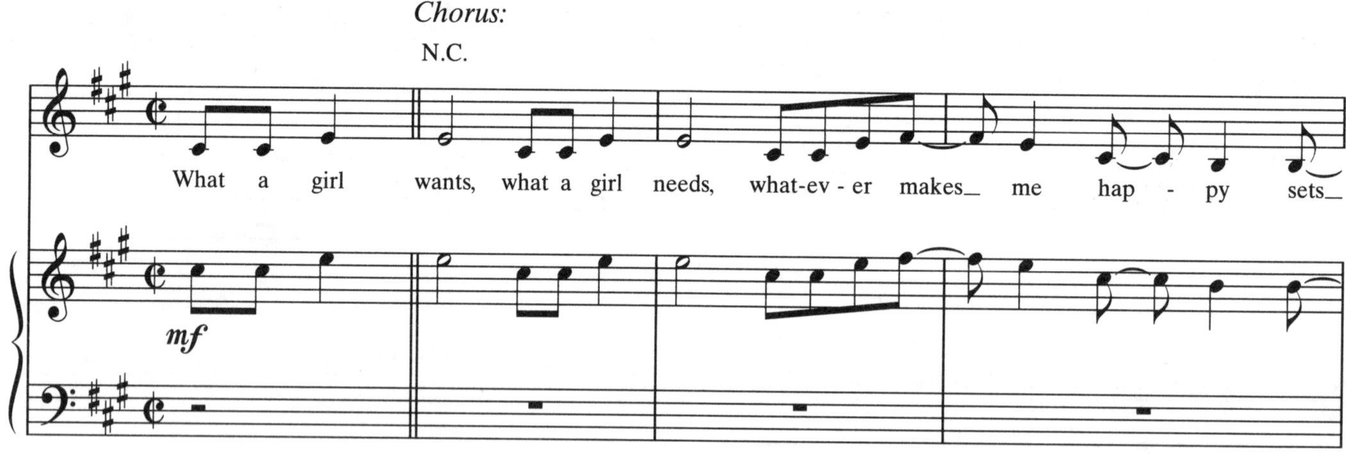

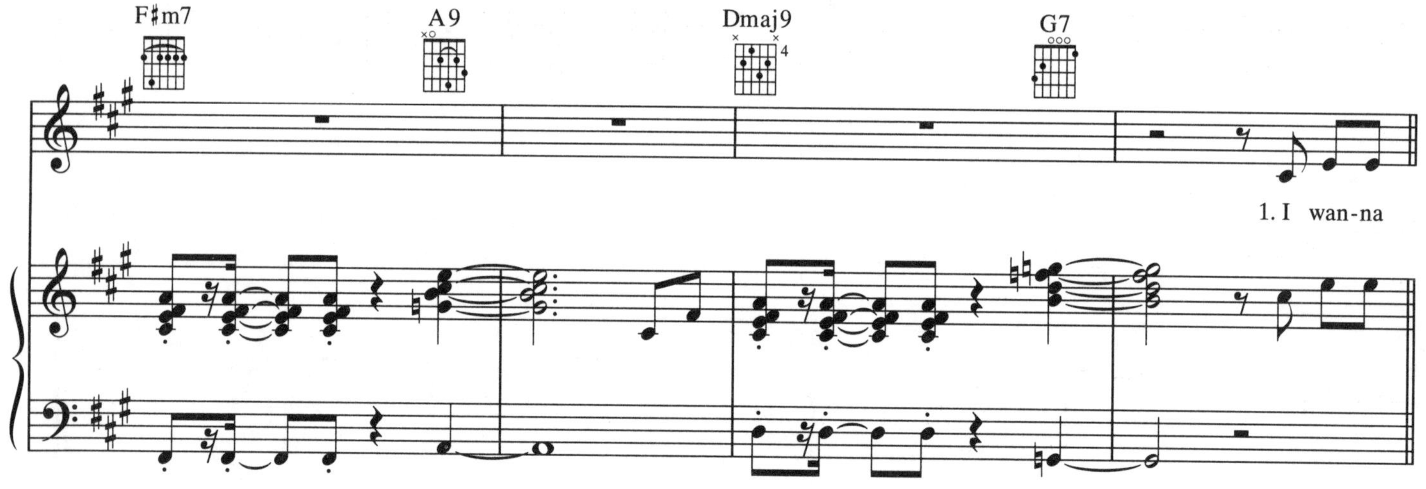

Verse:
F♯m7
thank you for giv - ing me time to breathe. Like a rock, you wait -
2. See additional lyrics
ed so pa - tient - ly while I got it to - geth - er, hmm,
simile
while I fig - ured it out. I on - ly looked, but I nev - er touched
B m9
'cause in my heart was a pic - ture of us hold - in' hands, mak -

D/E
in' plans, and it's luck - y for me___ you un - der-stand. What a girl
Chorus:
A
E6
A13
wants, what a girl needs, what - ev - er makes___ me hap - py sets___
Dmaj7
Dm7
G7
___ you free,___ and I'm thank - ing you
for know - ing ex - act - ly.
for giv - ing it to me.
A
E6
A13
What a girl wants, what a girl needs, what - ev - er keeps___ me in___

Dmaj7
Dm7
G7
— your arms, — and I'm thank - ing you for be - ing there for me.
1.
F♯m7
A9
Dmaj9
G7
2.
F♯m7
A9
2. A weak-er Oh, ba - by. Oh, dar - lin',
Dmaj9
G13
Bridge:
F♯m7
C♯m7
thank — you, thank — you. A girl needs some-bod - y

A9 Dmaj7

sen - si - tive__ but tough,________ some-bod - y there__ when the go - in' gets

F♯m7 C♯m7 A9 D7

rough. Ev - er - y night__ he'll be giv - ing his love______ to just one

F♯m7 C♯m7

girl,__ one girl,__ one.______ Some-bod - y cool__ but real ten - der

C♯m
hang - in' a - round with the one who al - ways knew... What a girl
Chorus:
A
E6
A13
wants, what a girl needs, what - ev - er makes me hap - py sets
Dmaj7
Dm7
G9
A
E6
you free. (Lead vocal ad lib.) What a girl wants, what a girl needs,
A13
Dmaj7
Dm7
G7
what - ev - er keeps me in your arms. What a girl

Chorus:
A
E6
A13
wants, what a girl needs, what-ev-er makes me hap-py sets
Dmaj7
Dm7
G7
you free, and I'm thank-ing you for giv-ing it to me.
A
E6
A13
What a girl wants, what a girl needs, what-ev-er keeps me in
Dmaj7
Dm7
G7
your arms, and I'm thank-ing you for be-ing there. What a girl

Verse 2:
A weaker man might have walked away, but you had faith,
Strong enough to move over and give me space
While I got it together,
While I figured it out.
They say if you love something, let it go;
If it comes back, it's yours.
That's how you know it's for keeps, yeah, it's for sure,
And you're ready and willin' to give me more than…
(To Chorus:)

WHEN SOMETHING IS WRONG WITH MY BABY

Words and Music by
ISAAC HAYES and DAVID PORTER

Verse 2:
He: Just what she means to me now,
Oh, you just wouldn't understand.
People can say that she's no good,
But ah, she's my woman and I know I'm her man.
She: And if he's got a problem,
Oh, I know I got to help him solve 'em.
Both: When something is wrong with my baby,
Something is wrong with me.

WHERE'S THE LOVE

Words and Music by
ISAAC HANSON, TAYLOR HANSON,
ZACHARY HANSON, MARK HUDSON
and STEVEN SALOVER

Dm7
F
C
ing on and I don't know what it is, woh.
what you see when-ev-er you look a-round?
G
Dm7
F
You don't mind the tak-ing, girl, but you don't know how to give.
We're trip-ping all o-ver our-selves and pull-ing each oth-er down.
C
G/B
Am7
Bm7
Oh, you drove me cra-zy, but I don't know, ba-by.
Oh, we're sep-a-rat-ing, con-scious-ness is fad-ing.
C
Am7/D
Am7
You're think-ing that it's me you're fool-ing. Where's the right in

Bm7
Am7/D
all of our fight-ing? Look at what you're / we're do - ing.
Chorus:
G
F(9)
C7
Where's the love? It's not e-nough. It makes the world go
F
G
F(9)
'round and 'round and 'round. Where's the love? Give / Just give it up.
C7
1. E♭
F
G
It makes the world go 'round and 'round and 'round.

2.
E♭
F
'round and 'round_ and 'round.__
G
D/F♯
Bridge:
E7
Dark clouds all a - round,_ light - ning, rain pour - ing down._
Am
E7
We're wait - ing for the bright light to break through. Face down on the ground,_
F
G
pick us up__ at the lost and found. We've got to change our point of view_ if we want the sky blue._

A
E
G
(Inst. solo ad lib....
1.
2.
D
A
D
A/C♯
Bm7
...end solo) Oh, we're seg - re - gat - ing,
C♯m7
D
A/E
con - scienc - es are fad - ing. You're think - ing that it's me you're fool - ing, yeah.
Bm7
C♯m7
A/E
Where's the right in all of our fight - ing? Look at what

A
G(9)
we're do - ing.
Where's the love?
It's not e-nough.
D
G
A
It makes the world go
'round and 'round and 'round.
'round and 'round and 'round and 'round.
Where's the love?
G(9)
1.2.3.
D7
F
G
Just give it up.
It makes the world go
'round and 'round and 'round.
4.
D7
F
G
A
Won't you, won't you give it up?

YOU WERE MEANT FOR ME

G/B
C
D
pan-cakes, too,
I've got ma-ple syr-up,
ev-'ry - thing but
you.
C (9)
G/B
C
I break the yolks and make a
smil - y
face,
I kind of like it in my
Em
C (9)
G/B
brand new
place.
I wipe the
spots a - bove the mirror, don't leave the
keys in the
door.
I
Chorus:
C
D
C
nev - er put wet towels
on the
floor an - y - more, 'cause...
Dreams last
for

D
G
D/F♯
Em7
G/D
so long,
e - ven af - ter you're gone.
C
D
G
D/F♯
I know
you love me and
soon you will see
Em7
G/D
C
To Coda
1.
D
you were meant for me
and I was meant for you.
Em
2.
D
I was meant for

Bridge:
Em
Am7
you.
I go a-bout my bus-'ness, I'm
D
Bm
D
Em7
do - in' fine.__ Be-sides, what__ would I say__ if I had__ you on the line?
Am7
D
Bm7
Em
Same old sto - ry, not much to say. Hearts are bro-ken ev - 'ry day.__
C (9)
G/B
C
Em
D.S.𝄋 al Coda

Verse 2:
I called my mama, she was out for a walk.
Consoled a cup of coffee, but it didn't wanna talk.
So I picked up a paper, it was more bad news,
More hearts being broken or people being used.
Put on my coat in the pouring rain.
I saw a movie, it just wasn't the same,
'Cause it was happy and I was sad,
And it made me miss you, oh, so bad.
(To Chorus:)

Verse 3:
I brush my teeth and put the cap back on,
I know you hate it when I leave the light on.
I pick a book up and then I turn the sheets down,
And then I take a breath and a good look around.
Put on my pj's and hop into bed.
I'm half alive but I feel mostly dead.
I try and tell myself it'll be all right,
I just shouldn't think anymore tonight.
(To Chorus:)

(GOD MUST HAVE SPENT) A LITTLE MORE TIME ON YOU

Words and Music by
CARL STURKEN and EVAN ROGERS

F
Dm7
E♭
life was com - plete. I thought it was whole. Why do I feel like I'm los -
B♭
E♭
B♭
ing con - trol? 1.3. Nev - er thought that love could feel like this. And you
E♭
B♭
E♭
changed my world with just one kiss. How can it be that right
D
E♭
Fsus
F
here with me there's an an - gel? It's a mir - a - cle. Your
cresc.

Chorus:
B♭
E♭
F
Gm7
love is like a riv - er, peace - ful and deep. Your
mf
soul is like a se - cret that I could nev - er keep.
When I look in - to your eyes I know that it's true,
To Coda
1.
A♭
B♭/D
God must have spent a lit - tle more time on you.

F
Gm7
B♭
E♭
2.
On you, on you, on you,
you.
you.
3. Nev - er
D.S. 𝄋 al Coda

Coda

B♭ E♭ F Gm7

On you, on you, on you, you.

A♭ Gm7 B♭/D F E♭2

God must have spent a lit - tle more time on you,

a tempo

Fsus F E♭2 Fsus F B♭

a lit-tle more time on you.

rit.

Verse 2:
In all of creation,
All things great and small,
You are the one that surpasses them all.
More precious than
Any diamond or pearl;
They broke the mold
When you came in this world.
And I'm trying hard to figure it out,
Just how I ever did without
The warmth of your smile.
The heart of a child
That's deep inside,
Leaves me purified.
(To Chorus:)

WARNER BROS. PUBLICATIONS

BEST SELLING FOLIOS

THE GREATEST POP HITS OF 1999 SO FAR

(MF9913)

A collection of the greatest pop songs from the first half of 1999. *Titles (and artists) include:* All I Have to Give (Backstreet Boys) • Angel of Mine (Monica) • ...Baby One More Time (Britney Spears) • Believe (Cher) • Crush (Jennifer Paige) • Duel of the Fates (from *Star Wars: Episode I The Phantom Menace*) (John Williams) and more.

GREATEST COUNTRY HITS OF 1999 SO FAR

(MF9914)

A collection of the best country music from the first half of 1999. Features artists such as Garth Brooks, Faith Hill, George Strait, Clint Black, Alan Jackson, Steve Wariner, Tim McGraw, Shania Twain, Billy Ray Cyrus, Vince Gill, and more. *Titles include:* Burnin' the Roadhouse Down • Fly (The Angel Song) • From This Moment On • Hole in the Floor of Heaven • It's Your Song • Love Ain't Like That.

SMASH POP HITS 1998-1999

(MF9903)

Thirty-three top songs. *Titles (and artists) include:* All My Life (K-Ci & JoJo) • Angel of Mine (Monica) •...Baby One More Time (Britney Spears) • Crush (Jennifer Paige) • From This Moment On (Shania Twain) • Hands (Jewel) • I Don't Want to Miss a Thing (Aerosmith) • I'm Your Angel (R. Kelly & Celine Dion) • One Week (Barenaked Ladies) • Ray of Light (Madonna) • This Kiss (Faith Hill) • When the Lights Go Out (Five) and more.

THE GREATEST LOVE SONGS OF THE 90s

(MF9902)

Fifty-seven hit love songs from the world's top artists. *Titles (and artists) include:* I'm Your Angel (R. Kelly & Celine Dion) • Me and You (Kenny Chesney) • More Than Words (Extreme) • You Were Meant for Me (Jewel) • You're Still the One (Shania Twain) • This Kiss (Faith Hill) • Valentine (Jim Brickman) • All My Life (K-Ci and JoJo) • Because You Loved Me (Celine Dion) • How Do I Live (LeAnn Rimes) • Dreaming of You (Selena) and more.

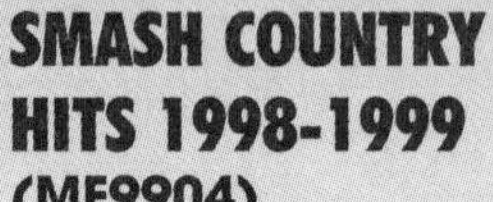

(MF9904)

Forty top songs *Titles (and artists) include*: Holes in the Floor of Heaven (Steve Wariner) • From This Moment On (Shania Twain) • This Kiss (Faith Hill) • 26¢ (The Wilkinsons) • There's Your Trouble (Dixie Chicks)• Loosen Up My Strings (Clint Black) • If You Ever Have Forever in Mind (Vince Gill) • It's Your Song (Garth Brooks) • You're Easy on the Eyes (Terri Clark) • It Must Be Love (Ty Herndon) and many more!

SMASH POP HITS 1999-2000 Special Edition

(MF9929)

Titles (and artists) include: All Star (Smash Mouth) • As Long As You Love Me (Backstreet Boys) • Back at One (Brian McKnight) • (You Drive Me) Crazy (Britney Spears) • From This Moment On (Shania Twain) • Genie in a Bottle (Christina Aguilera) • I Will Remember You (Sarah McLachlan) • (God Must Have Spent) A Little More Time on You (*NSYNC) • No Scrubs (TLC) • She's All I Ever Had (Ricky Martin) and many more.

SMASH COUNTRY HITS 1999-2000 Special Edition

(MF9928)

Titles (and artists) include: Almost Home (Mary Chapin Carpenter) • Anyone Else (Collin Raye) • Big Deal (LeAnn Rimes) • Come on Over (Shania Twain) • Give My Heart to You (Billy Ray Cyrus) • Her (Aaron Tippin) • Holes in the Floor of Heaven (Steve Wariner) • It Don't Matter to the Sun (Garth Brooks as Chris Gaines) and many, many more.

The Best Personality Folios of 1999

CHRISTINA AGUILERA
(PF9927) Piano/Vocal/Chords

BACKSTREET BOYS
(PF9731A) Piano/Vocal/Chords
Millennium
(PF9916) Piano/Vocal/Chords

GARTH BROOKS
Double Live
(PF9906) Piano/Vocal/Chords

CELINE DION
All The Way... A Decade of Song
(0437B) Piano/Vocal/Chords
Let's Talk About Love
(PF9813) Piano/Vocal/Chords

JEWEL
Spirit
(PF9836) Piano/Vocal/Chords
(PG9810) Guitar/Vocal with Tablature

KID ROCK
Devil Without A Cause
(0422B) Authentic Guitar-Tab Edition

KORN
Issues
(PGM0001) Authentic Guitar-Tab Edition

LIMP BIZKIT
Three Dollar Bill
(PG9901) Authentic Guitar-Tab Edition

LIVE
The Distance to Here
(PG9911) Authentic Guitar-Tab Edition

***NSYNC**
(PF9908) Piano/Vocal/Chords

RAGTIME
Vocal Selections
(5206A) Piano/Vocal/Chords

SANTANA
Supernatural
(0413B) Authentic Guitar-Tab Edition

BRITNEY SPEARS
...Baby One More Time
(PF9911) Piano/Vocal/Chords

STAR WARS
Episode I: The Phantom Menace
(0347B) Piano/Vocal/Chords

SHANIA TWAIN
Come on Over
(PF9746) Piano/Vocal/Chords

KENNY WAYNE SHEPARD
Live On
(PG9909) Authentic Guitar-Tab Edition

Printed in USA AD 0137A 01/00